How to Build an Evangelistic Church Music Program

How to Build

an Evangelistic

Church Music

Program

LINDSAY TERRY

THOMAS NELSON INC.
NASHVILLE / NEW YORK

Library of Congress Cataloging in Publication Data

Terry, Lindsay.
   How to build an evangelistic church music program.

   1. Church music. I. Title.
MT88.T465H6   783'.026   74–14658
ISBN 0–8407–5581–3

To the Adult Choir of
the Northside Baptist
Church, Charlotte, North
Carolina, a faithful core
of musicians dedicated to
the service of Christ.

Contents

Preface

IN writing this book I have tried to develop a manual that may be followed by the music director of any size church to build a good *evangelistic* music program.

The ideas and methods set down on the following pages are, for the most part, not theories but workable suggestions, tried and proven through the years. They have been used in building music programs for such great churches as the Northwest Baptist Church in Miami, Florida; the Salem Baptist Church in Winston-Salem, North Carolina; the First Baptist Church in Hammond, Indiana; Marietta (Georgia) Baptist Tabernacle; and the Northside Baptist Church, Charlotte, North Carolina.

Because I believe a church's music program should be heart-warming and easily understood, the entire book is written with that in mind.

The church service is the showcase or focal point of all of the music activity. A great deal of money and countless hours are spent in preparation for this time; therefore, the major portion of this book deals with the methods used in planning, rehearsing, building and preparing for the church services.

Doubtless no church can use all of the ideas exactly as presented, but if some can be helpfully used, in any form, I will be elated and blessed to know it.

LINDSAY TERRY
Charlotte, North Carolina

Introduction

THERE is no great New Testament church that is not a singing church. When I wrote the books *The Ten Largest Sunday Schools* and *America's Fastest Growing Churches,* I noted that their music was different from the typical American church. I heard Lindsay Terry say, "Church music comes from Bible doctrine." I knew what he meant, that a New Testament church must have New Testament music. The purpose of a church is to win people to Jesus Christ. A church music program is aimed at directing people to Jesus Christ.

I noted in the books on large churches that they had happy music, because the New Testament produces happy people. The Bible word is "blessed," which means happy. Blessed is the church that has a happy song, for they shall lead others to the Lord.

Music is the spiritual thermostat of a church, being both a regulator and reflector of the temperature. First, a thermostat incorporates a thermometer, which simply tells the heat level in a room. When I walk into a church that has nothing but classical anthems, I usually find no soul-winning activity. (There is nothing wrong with classical music, but it does not communicate to the heart of twentieth-century Americans; as a matter of fact, it turns them off, hence turning them away from God.)

Second, a thermostat regulates the furnace, hence the music can motivate people to soul winning and service. Use the ideas of his book to bring revival to your church. The author is extremely practical in such topics as how to select music, platform appearance, how to enlist musicians, and how to direct the program. Correctly applied, this book could be the instrument of revival for your church.

As important as music is, it is not the whole program of the church. Do not be deceived to think that correct music alone will bring revival to your church, for revival comes through agonizing prayer, Bible teaching, and serious Christian service. Harold Henniger, pastor, Canton Baptist Temple, best stated the balance: "You can't build a great church on music, but you can't build a great church *without* music."

The author is at once both profound and simple. His thoughts are so deep that you will have to read some paragraphs many times to understand the implications for your church. But, at the same time, you will find this a simple book, for music is simply opening the heart's door and expressing one's feeling in song. Music is the soul's expression.

I think Lindsay Terry is one of the best church musicians in America. I have been on the platform when he has led music programs, and I am amazed at his talents. I saw him lead members of the Atlanta Symphony Orchestra at the Regency Hyatt House for one of the most beautiful church banquets at which I have spoken. Lindsay Terry was dignified in his tuxedo and pulled expression from the musicians that moved our hearts. I have also heard him lead singing at a pastors' conference, motivating four thousand pastors. I am glad this artist has attempted to put his soul on paper, and I hope that you capture his expertise by reading this book.

Evangelistic music inspires me, even though I have a "tin ear." My children say I even talk flat. I once tried to sing in a quartet; and one summer I led singing in an evangelistic tent. I wanted to be a musician, but finally realized I did not have musical talent. God has given to Lindsay Terry the talent of music. His music speaks to my heart. I should go a step further and say that his music thrills me, for he can do what I can't. Even though I can't sing, I love to sing. And even though I can't play an instrument, I wish I could. I like the response this man pulls from me through his music.

May God set your heart to singing and, as you read the pages of this book, inspire you to "make a joyful noise unto the Lord."

ELMER L. TOWNS

1

Music in the Bible

MUSIC is the universal language of mankind, and God is the author of this language. The Bible first mentions music early in the writings God gave through Moses: Genesis 4:20, "Jubal . . . was the father of all such as handle the harp and organ." God intended that music should bless, thrill, encourage, calm—and be enjoyed by—man; and man is to use music to help others. He is to teach and admonish his fellowman with song. "Let the word of Christ dwell in you richly in all wisdom; teaching and admonishing one another in psalms and hymns and spiritual songs, singing with grace in your hearts to the Lord" (Col. 3:16).

Music in the Old Testament

Man is to praise God in song. God declared to Job (38:7) that there was a time "when the morning stars sang together, and all the sons of God shouted for joy." God questioned Job as to his knowledge of him. Each one who comes to know God through his Son finds a song in his heart; God causes the sons of men on earth to sing together in praise to him.

The Song of Moses and the Children of Israel

Moses and the children of Israel sang together after God delivered them from bondage; their song is recorded in Exodus 15:1–19. Their joyful, victorious hearts were moved to singing. The same is true today.

The Psalms of David

The Book of Psalms is the hymnbook of the Bible. Written, for the most part, by David, the psalms seem to be a kind of folk song given to men in times of trouble, oppression, and deliverance.

Before leaving the Old Testament, consider an occasion that would certainly have been a joy to witness: II Chronicles 5:13 says, "It came even to pass, as the trumpeters and singers were as one, to make one sound to be heard in praising and thanking the Lord; and when they lifted up their voice with the trumpets and cymbals and instruments of musick, and praised the Lord, saying, For he is good; for His mercy endureth for ever. . . ."

Music in the New Testament

Music plays a wonderful role in the New Testament. Perhaps the first song came early at the birth of Christ. The angels may have "sung" together the message of his wondrous birth, although the Bible does not say this.

Singing of Jesus

Jesus sang as a child, at the usual gatherings for children or perhaps at school. He sang with his disciples—perhaps only once, but at least once. Matthew 26:30 says, "And when they had sung an hymn, they went out into the mount of Olives." He had been with his disciples during the Last Supper. He had blessed and broken the bread, had given thanks, and had passed the bread and wine to them. After they had eaten, they sang—sang a song of praise to God.

Singing in the Early Churches

Christians in the early church sang. Paul wrote to the church at Corinth, "I will sing with the spirit and I will sing with the understanding also." He also wrote to the church at Colosse the exhortation given earlier in this chapter. In numerous other places Christian singing is mentioned.

Singing in the Revelation

In the last book of the Bible are these words: "And they sing the song of Moses the servant of God, and the song of the Lamb, saying, Great and marvellous are thy works, Lord God Almighty; just and true are thy ways, thou King of saints. Who shall not fear thee, O Lord, and glorify thy name? for thou only art holy: for all nations shall come and worship before thee; for thy judgments are made manifest" (Rev. 15:3–4).

Christian singing is based on the Scriptures.

2

Evangelistic Music

PASTORS across America cry for a musical program that is vibrant and heartwarming, a music program that *lives* as it projects a message of life. Never has there been such need for music that moves upon the hearts of people as there is today; never such need for

music that the common man can grasp and understand;

music that speaks to the masses;

music that knows no boundary;

music enjoyed by the uneducated as well as the educated,

the poor and the rich,

the high and the low,

the children and the adults,

the teens and the grandparents . . .

The sacred classics are beautiful, and they should have a time and place in every life; but an evangelistic church service is not the time or the place. Consider these three reasons.

1. *The classics tend to call attention to the performance.* All too often the real message of the composition becomes lost in great swelling chords and oft-repeated phrases. The actual make-up of the composition becomes dominant. This glorifies the song and

not the Savior. Every Christian musical presentation should leave the audience more aware of the message of the song than of the excellence of the performance—not that both should not be favorably accepted.

2. *The classics lend themselves to a formal service.* Formalism and evangelism do not go hand in hand. Formalism soothes and deadens; evangelism arouses and awakens. A pastor cannot expect to arouse to positive action a congregation lulled into complacency by the musical portion of the service. Congregations, generally speaking, are not deeply moved by the sacred classics.

3. *The classics are too difficult for the ordinary church choir to sing well.* Since most choirs, especially in smaller churches, are made up of relatively untrained singers, few of them are able to master the classics. A choir should not perform in a service any music that cannot be learned well. Nothing distresses pastor and congregation more than to hear the pitiful struggles of an ill-prepared choir. With time at a premium and rehearsal time limited, it is far better to use music the singers can learn rapidly and perform well. They will then take personal pride in the choir and their part in the service. This is a *must* for an evangelistic atmosphere.

The classics should certainly be used and appreciated, but in a special program or concert in which they can be presented for audience appreciation of both composition and performance.

The music program of any church should be given as thorough care as humanly possible. Evangelistic music can be done in a way that will challenge the best musicians, and still be understood and enjoyed by the entire audience.

To further define evangelistic music, consider the following characteristics.

It Tells a Story

Many songs relate a story or are in story form. These are effective because they are usually filled with human interest. Everyone loves a story, and stories set to music are retained in the mind more readily. Some story-songs are: "Then Jesus Came," "The Stranger of Galilee," "At Calvary," "The Old Rugged Cross," and "Christ Arose." The most effective of these are based on the Scriptures, as opposed to others with only "religious flavor."

It Gives a Testimony

Truly some of the most blessed songs are those that bear testimony of faith in the Savior. Songs of testimony have been used to bring many people to a knowledge of Christ. These songs, like all others in the services, must have a definite quality of sincerity. Some of these are: "A Child of the King," "When I Get to the End of the Way," "Saved! Saved!," "Since I Have Been Redeemed," "Standing on the Promises," "The Solid Rock," "Amazing Grace," "Each Step I Take," and "Jesus Gives Me a Song." The titles indicate that songs of testimony are favorites of people across America and have been used of God to touch the hearts of countless people.

It Is a Prayer

Many best-loved songs and hymns are prayers set to music. A whole congregation can pray together by singing a prayer. A prayer song is always addressed to the Heavenly Father, to Jesus Christ, or to the Holy Spirit. The music director or the pastor should occasionally remind the congregation to think of the words they are singing. It must hurt the heart of God for his people to be praying to him in the words of a song and yet hardly knowing what they are asking of him or what they are saying to him. Polls taken across America show that high on the list of favorite songs are some that are prayers set to music. One is "Rock of Ages." Other songs that would be considered prayers are "Savior, Like a Shepherd Lead Us," "Love Divine," "I Am Thine, O Lord," "I Need Thee Every Hour," "Pass Me Not, O Gentle Savior," "My Faith Looks Up to Thee," and "Take My Life and Let It Be."

It Teaches

One of the grandest uses of sacred music is in teaching people —men, women, boys and girls—the things of God. From preschool years in the Sunday school and on through life, people are taught the truths of God through sacred song. One reason that songs are such good teachers is that people hear them over and over again. Repetition is like mucilage: it seals and causes a message to stick in the minds of those who take part in the singing. Many a wayward person has come to the Lord Jesus Christ later in life because he remembered a song his godly mother had sung many years before. He had been taught of God through song.

People cannot be taught through sacred music unless it carries a definite message or lesson. The following songs have wonderful messages needed by every person: "There Is a Fountain Filled with Blood," "Though Your Sins Be as Scarlet," and "Calvary Covers It All." These songs are usually sung by young people and adults; but Sunday school for little tots would not be nearly as effective without the "little" songs through which children learn.

It Praises

There is a distinction between hymns and gospel songs. A hymn is a song of praise to Jesus, the Heavenly Father, or the Holy Spirit. Although many people lump all sacred songs into one category—hymns—this is not technically correct. The gospel song tells a story or gives a message of some kind, and a hymn is directed to God.

Much is said in the Bible about praising God with the voice as well as with instruments. In Colossians 3:16, Paul seems to make a distinction between songs and hymns. The author believes that the "hymns" spoken of are songs of praise to God, while the "spiritual songs" mentioned are songs with a spiritual message or testimony or prayer.

Many hymns of praise are evangelistic in scope, for example: "All Hail the Power of Jesus' Name," "O For a Thousand Tongues to Sing," "Glory to His Name," "Praise Him, Praise Him," "O

Come, All Ye Faithful," "The Name of Jesus," and "How Great Thou Art." Just as the prayer song "Rock of Ages" rates high in the polls taken in America, "How Great Thou Art," a song of praise, is also highly favored among those polled.

It Expresses Love

God looks on the heart, and an expression of love in any form is acceptable to him. In my opinion the most beautiful way to express love to the Savior is through songs—usually prayer songs, although every prayer song is not necessarily a song of love.

Consider the following songs of love: "Lead Me to Some Soul Today" (a song that shows love for the lost), "O Love That Wilt Not Let Me Go," "Love Lifted Me," "Sunlight," and "Jesus Loves Even Me."

Surely, a most beautiful sight to the Savior is a group of his people, gathered together with bowed heads and sincere hearts, singing,

> My Jesus, I Love Thee, I know Thou art mine,
> For Thee all the follies of sin I resign.
> My gracious Redeemer, my Savior art Thou;
> If ever I loved Thee, my Jesus, 'tis now.

It Warns

Songs that warn of judgment to come are not beautiful songs, nor are they enjoyable to sing, but they need to be used occasionally. They do not bless the hearts of Christians as other songs, but they still need to be sung. Words of warning to those without Christ or to those living afar from God stay in the mind longer, perhaps, because they are usually set to a haunting melody. In many cases, the combination of the words and the melody causes the song to reach great heights. Songs of warning are not as numerous as others, but consider a few: "The Great Judgment Morning," "Have You Counted the Cost?," "There's a Great Day Coming," and "Ye Must Be Born Again."

It Anticipates

Songs of anticipation are songs about heaven, Christ's return, or his eternal reign. Every Christian should continually anticipate the coming of Christ, when we shall be with him. Songs about heaven should not be reserved for funerals, but should be used often in services and in daily lives. The following songs are songs of anticipation: "Zion's Hill," "Christ Returneth," "One Day," "What if It Were Today?," "After," "At the End of the Road," "We Shall See His Lovely Face," and "When I Get to the End of the Way."

It Assures

Sacred music would not be complete without songs of assurance that help Christians to know their salvation is steadfast, and to be sure that God sees, knows, and cares for them. Singing in time of trial or darkness brightens any situation, reminding people that God is still on the throne. It is grand and glorious to sing in the midst of trouble, even as Paul and Silas sang, with bleeding backs and feet in the stocks.

"The cross it standeth fast. . . ." Christians are helped by being reminded in song of this truth, especially in times of doubt or trouble. These words open the song "Hallelujah for the Cross." Other songs of assurance are "Blessed Assurance," "A Shelter in the Time of Storm," "He Leadeth Me," "I Must Tell Jesus," and "Jesus, Savior, Pilot Me."

It Blesses

Singing, or hearing a song beautifully sung, has brought me the greatest thrills or blessings. No thrill or blessing has exceeded that of hearing "The Loveliness of Christ" sung by a blind singer. Music in evangelistic church services is marvelous in its blessing to those who hear or who take part as congregation or special singers. While church music should chiefly be geared to help reach the lost, it should also be for the blessing and strength for the saved.

Of the thousands of songs in this category, here are a few: "Jesus Is All the World to Me," "How Firm a Foundation," "Jesus, the Very Thought of Thee," "The Name of Jesus," and "All Things in Jesus."

It Comforts

Many elderly people, especially, find comfort in wonderful sacred songs that tell of heaven. Others, not so elderly, find comfort and strength in such songs as "Safe in the Arms of Jesus," "Lead Me Gently Home," "I Must Tell Jesus," "Blest Be the Tie that Binds," "Does Jesus Care?," God Understands," "I Never Walk Alone," "From Every Stormy Wind That Blows," and "No One Ever Cared for Me Like Jesus." A world filled with sorrow, heartache, and toil would suffer a great loss if deprived of these or the thousands of other wonderful songs of comfort.

It Prepares

Life on earth is a continual preparation. The Christian's greatest task, besides winning others to Christ, is preparing to spend eternity with God. Christians fail here perhaps more than in any other area. Not only is there a lack of preparation for heaven, but also there is a lack of preparation for serving God here on the earth. Examples of songs that would prepare Christians for the work of God or for a home in heaven are "Where He Leads Me," "Break Thou the Bread of Life," "Faith Is the Victory," "I Surrender All," "Beneath the Cross of Jesus," and "More Like the Master."

It Gives An Invitation

The most important time in an evangelistic service is the invitation time. The songs have been sung, the Scriptures have been read, the announcements have been given, prayer has been made, and the sermon has been delivered. Then comes the time of invitation—the time when men are invited to come and make a public profession of faith in the Lord Jesus. Songs that can be used at this time are "Just As I Am" (probably the most popular invitation song ever written), "Softly and Tenderly," "Jesus, I Come," "Why Do You Wait?," "Jesus Is Calling," "Only Trust Him," "Jesus Calls Us," and "Come Unto Me."

If any song in the service is to be sung with sincerity and a full realization of its words, the song of invitation after the sermon is that song. Lives seem literally to hang in the balance. God is moving upon hearts. People hear the inviting song, and are moved to do as it bids.

It Exhorts

One of the most famous of all hymn stories is that behind "Stand Up, Stand Up for Jesus," a song of exhortation. This song was born in a time of revival, when Dudley Tyng lay dying after a horrible accident. At that time his exhortation to the young men who had worked with him as "Stand up for Jesus." Out of this tragedy was born "Stand Up, Stand Up for Jesus." Another wonderful song of exhortation, "We're Marching to Zion," starts out commandingly, "Come, we that love the Lord." Accompanied by the martial rhythm, it grips the hearts of people and moves them toward God. Other songs of exhortation are "Onward, Christian Soldiers," "Tell It to Jesus," and "Go, Tell It on the Mountain." Songs of exhortation move God's people to action —or, at least, intend to do so. God help it to be so!

It Expresses Gratitude

If God's people have any fault more continually with them than others, it is ungratefulness. This attitude could be changed through congregational use of such songs as "O Happy Day," "Thank You, Jesus," "Come, Ye Thankful People, Come," or "Count Your Blessings."

American people have been blessed as no other people on the

face of the earth. How thankful God's people in America ought to be. Songs of gratitude should be a regular part of our church services.

It Strengthens

In these days, and in the days that lie ahead, Christians can find help in singing songs that call their attention to the strength that God gives. Hundreds of songs, perhaps even thousands, do this, but consider these few: "Dare to Be a Daniel," "Deeper and Deeper," "If I Gained the World," "In Times Like These," "The Old-Fashioned Home," and "When I Kneel Down to Pray."

Evangelistic music does all of the things discussed here and more. Considered collectively or individually, evangelistic songs are what the people of America need. Since this is true, it behooves every church to make her music program evangelistic.

The following are thoughts concerning church music by two of America's greatest pastors, Dr. Lee Roberson, Highland Park Baptist Church, Chattanooga, Tennessee, and Dr. Jack Hyles, First Baptist Church, Hammond, Indiana, (which boasts America's largest Sunday school).

THE CHURCH MUSICIAN AND HIS MUSIC
by Lee Roberson

It is a delight for me to write on the subject of church music. I have been preaching for almost forty-five years, but have had an intense interest in music from the time of my conversion. I remember the first song that I led, in the old Cedar Creek Baptist Church in Louisville, Kentucky. I remember the battles I had between preaching and singing in the early part of my ministry. I had such delight in singing that I felt this was the ministry God had for me. But no, God had a definite purpose for my life, and I rejoice that I accepted his way.

What a great calling is that of music! How marvelously God uses men and women in the proclamation of divine truth through music.

The music director of any church—large or small—should give his best to the calling that is his. He should seek the best training possible, both as a vocalist and as a director. Homer Rodeheaver, who became world famous as a soloist and song leader for Billy Sunday, was still taking voice lessons at seventy-five. He was ever striving to be his best for the glory of God.

So it should be for every singer, and for you. Get the best in training. Know music. Let the learning process continue throughout life. Good teachers are available in most cities. It costs money to take lessons, but it is worth it.

Not only should you as a music director know music, but you must know people. Some leaders fail at this point. They know music—they are technically well-trained—but they cannot work with others. Study people. Study the methods for producing the best of music from poor "sinners saved by grace."

The building of a great choir is dependent upon the leader and his ability. He must stir others, and he must challenge them to give their best. Good leadership solves the problem of attendance and also the problem of producing God-glorifying music.

There is so much to be said upon this subject that I prefer to outline briefly what I think music should do. I am referring to the greatest of all music—sacred music.

1. *Music should inspire.* Music should inspire us to noble living. The proper kind of music should cause us to hate lowly, sinful things and encourage us to strive for the noblest life.

Music should inspire us to a dedication of life. How many of us would have to testify that we have come to the place of dedication through the message of a well-selected and properly presented song?

Music should inspire us to service, unselfish service. Music, based upon the Word of God, should call forth our human best for his divine purposes.

2. *Music should encourage.* We all have times of discouragement. Despondency often besets us. David had some low, dark hours, but he had a song in his heart. Read the Psalms carefully; you will see the evidence of this. Fanny Crosby had lonely, discouraging hours. She never saw the light of day or the beauty of God's flowers or the loveliness of the sunset. Fanny Crosby received encouragement through her God, and her songs reveal this. Dr. Charles Weigle wrote his best songs in the times of his greatest gloom. "No One Ever Cared for Me Like Jesus" came out of a dark hour. "I Have Found A Hiding Place" came from a time of despondency.

As the songwriters found encouragement, even in difficult hours, to write songs, so we should find encouragement in music to lift us to higher planes in hours of dejection and despair.

I remember, when I first began my work as a preacher, the blessedness of the song "Just When I Need Him Most." Down through the years, this song has ever given me encouragement.

3. *Music should teach.* Yes, music should teach us the love of God, salvation by grace, eternal security, justification by faith, the second coming of Christ, heaven, and hell; and the great doctrines of the Word should be made plain through our songs.

There is something wrong with a song that teaches nothing. (We had better check some of the modern-day sacred songs. Many of them teach nothing at all.) Bible teaching must be interwoven in all sacred gospel songs and hymns.

4. *Music should ever point to the Savior.* Yes, "faith cometh by hearing, and hearing by the word of God." But as songs are based upon the Word of God, they will have the message to aid people to see Christ.

Many of the simple songs that we sing so often express the thought I have in mind. I refer to songs like "My Faith Looks Up to Thee," "Amazing Grace, How Sweet the Sound," "My Hope Is Built on Nothing Less Than Jesus' Blood and Righteousness," and "What Can Wash Away My Sin? Nothing but the Blood of Jesus." The Word of God can be preached through songs, as well as through the spoken Word. We must use in our churches songs that will continually place before sinners Christ, the only Savior. The beauty of melody must sometimes be sacrificed for a song with a definite, pointed emphasis on Christ Jesus.

Yes, music should inspire; music should encourage; music should teach; and music should point to Christ the Savior! I am sure there is much more that can be said upon this subject, but I am merely touching what I feel is primary. Every church should seek to present the finest and the best in music Sunday after Sunday. This requires time, money, energy, and dedication. It requires death to self, the filling of the Spirit, and a constant looking-up for divine approval.

Now, permit me to close these comments with two verses from the Word of God: "Speaking to yourselves in psalms and hymns and spiritual songs, singing and making melody in your heart to the Lord; "Giving thanks always for all things unto God and the Father in the name of our Lord Jesus Christ" (Eph. 5:19, 20).

THE REAL NEED OF EVANGELISTIC MUSIC
by Jack Hyles

Music is one of the most important forms of praise. The word "hallelujah," which means "praise the Lord," is pronounced the same in all languages. The last five psalms begin and end with the words "Praise ye the Lord." In Psalm 74:21, the poor and needy are admonished to praise the Lord. In Psalm 148:12, the young and the old are to praise the Lord. In this same verse, men and women are to praise the Lord. In Psalm 71:14, David said he would praise the Lord more and more. Psalm 63:3 says, "My lips shall praise thee." Psalm 66:5, "Let all the people praise thee." Psalm 148:2, "Praise ye him, all his angels." Also in Psalm 148, the sun, moon, stars, dragons, fish, animals, hail, snow, and birds are commanded to praise him. David loved to use the words "Oh, that men might praise the Lord." Isaiah said in chapter 25, verse 1, "I will praise thy name." Jeremiah 33:11 says, "Praise the Lord of hosts." Paul and Silas praised him at midnight as they sang. In II Chronicles 29:30, the Levites sang praises to God. Peter admonishes us in I Peter 2:9 to show forth his praises.

In no way can we praise the Lord better and more sweetly than with music. A song was sung after the Israelites had crossed the Red Sea. When Deborah and Barak had defeated the forces of Sisera, a song was sung. Mary sang when she heard of the coming of the Christ child.

Once a man in my church who managed a cafeteria told me to visit his establishment at the noon hour. He instructed his organist to play a waltz. The people literally waltzed through and slowly picked up their food. Then he instructed her to play a march. The people very quickly and with jerky motions picked up their food. He said, "You see, Pastor, what influence music has on people." Because this is true, church music should influence people for the right. Dead music can tranquilize the audience before the sermon. For that matter, it can tranquilize the preacher. Rock music set to religious words can cause a service to turn toward the sensual. There is nothing more vital than proper music in the church, music that appeals to the heart, music that gives a message, music that is spiritual both in lyrics and in melody. May God use this publication to stabilize our churches musically.

3

The Pastor and

the Music Program

EVERY pastor has a definite role to play if his music program is to be successful. Too often pastors have the attitude, "Oh, well, I'll just leave the music up to the music director; he knows more about that than I do." As far as the technical end of the music program is concerned, this may be true; but every pastor should know more about what his people need, in the way of music, than anyone else. He does not have to be a musician, but every pastor should know enough about the musical needs of his congregation to help guide the music program.

The Bible indicates that God gives each pastor a special gift; he has not promised this gift to the music director. The music director does not know the real spiritual needs of a congregation, therefore he should depend on the pastor to give some direction in the music ministry of the church. Not that the pastor should plan in minute detail every aspect of the church music program, but he is to provide leadership in the music ministry of the church, as he does in every other area.

Two specific areas that need to be explored are discussed in this chapter.

The Pastor and the Music Director

Although many churches "call" the music director in much the same way as they do the pastor, the two are by no means partners. The pastor should have complete authority over the church and the music director. The music director should recognize this. It is biblical. Hebrews, chapter thirteen, is the basis for this viewpoint. Any music director who does not recognize the authority and position of the pastor is heading for serious trouble, and perhaps will cause severe difficulties. The pastor should not tolerate insubordination on the part of any staff member. This is not to say that the pastor is the more favored in the sight of the Lord, or better than the music director; but God has his plan, and his plan is for the pastor to lead the church and the people. The music director is part of the church and the people. May God have mercy on a music director who takes it upon himself to try to lead the people away from the pastor, dividing the church.

The loyalty of a music director to his pastor should be without question. Any criticism or casting of a shadow on some decision or act of the pastor by the music director is unthinkable. In fact, the music director should not even listen to other church members who belittle or criticize the pastor in any way. He should actively defend the pastor at all times. If he cannot do this, he should quietly and quickly resign and move to another location. On the other hand, any rumor about, or criticism of the music director should be discounted by the pastor until proven. The pastor should defend the music director at all times, and especially in the face of criticism or belittlement. Each should pray daily for the other.

Mutual Support in the Public Services

There should be a visible spirit of cooperation. This puts the audience at ease, and makes for harmony and a good spirit in the services.

Quite often the pastor will have occasion to refer to the music director in his sermon. This should be done in good taste—and should be received well on the part of the music director. This endears both men to the audience.

The music director should deliberately recognize the authority of the pastor in the services, and should cause the music to fit the personality of the pastor. The messages of a young, energetic pastor could be enhanced or augmented by a little more lively music program in general. (In some cases, a more subdued program might give a much needed change of pace.) On the other hand, if a pastor is prone to be reserved or quiet, a more lively song service and music program might balance the service.

In summary, each should do all in his power to enhance the ministry of the other.

Choosing a Full-time Music Director

1. *Finding a Candidate.* Possibly one of the most wide-open fields in Christianity today is that of the full-time music director. Most pastors and churches are looking for a "fancy Dan," who knows music but has no compassion for the lost or concern about being a real spiritual help to the church. Hundreds of churches across America need a good full-time music director who really wants to do a good job for the Savior. Real soul-winning music directors are the crying need.

Many churches have a personnel committee. Perhaps this committee is fine when it comes to hiring janitors or secretaries, but the hiring of a full-time music director should be led by the pastor. He is in a better position to find out who is available in this field. Because the music director plays such an important role in the service of the church, his selection must be kept upon a high spiritual plane. To any church, the choosing of a good music director is second in importance only to the choosing of a good pastor. This is another reason why the pastor should lead in this selection. As a general rule, it is best to consider someone already serving well in a church, unless a candidate who is just graduating from college or seminary is available. The author does not advocate deliberately pulling a music director away from another church, but many times a music director may feel that a change is of the Lord, although he is doing a good job at the church he is presently serving. Every good music director, it seems, is busy somewhere.

Smaller churches might do well to carefully consider an undergraduate of a good Christian school, who is being trained, and who needs practical experience, in this field to prepare him for future success. He can gain this training while still in school, coming to the church on the weekends or during the summer.

The most important aspect in finding a good music director is the leading of the Lord. Every church should pray diligently that God would direct them in choosing the right man for them. Too many churches have had severe trouble because they were lax in choosing the right music director. Considering this and the other points set down, it is evident that the pastor must lead in this important selection.

2. *Interviewing the Candidate.* After a likely candidate has been found, then the pastor, not the personnel committee, should interview the candidate first. They may want to talk to him, and the deacons may want to interview or question him, but the pastor should make the first contact and have the first interview with the candidate. This can be done either by telephone or in person; but a personal interview is most desirable in every case. Many questions can be answered to the satisfaction of both candidate and pastor at this first conference. First impressions are not always absolutely correct, but, many times, good rapport can be started at this point.

In this interview the pastor can obtain information about the candidate's training and personal background. Every music director should live in such a way that he would not fear to have his background explored by any committee or pastor of a church to which he may go. The pastor can, in the initial interview, acquaint the candidate with the kind of music program that he wants for his church, giving the candidate the opportunity to proceed or to gracefully back out, saving time and expense later on.

3. *Having the Candidate Visit the Church.* During the second

or third interview, the prospective music director should be invited to visit the church, on a weekend, so that he may spend time in rehearsal with the choir, and may direct the music during one or both Sunday services. This does not give the congregation adequate knowledge of his ability to direct the complete music program, but it does give them some exposure to him, and he to them. Although his past record will be the deciding factor, the visit to the church is invaluable.

4. *Understanding Policies and Duties.* One of the most predominant difficulties experienced by music directors is the lack of a clear understanding of the policies of the pastor or the church, and of his duties. Often music directors have more than one duty to perform, especially in smaller churches. The music director might also take care of the religious education. Many times his title is Director of Music and Education, or Director of Music and Youth. Occasionally, the music director is considered as assistant pastor, or assistant to the pastor. These dual titles or dual jobs are all the more reason for a definite understanding of the policies and duties before a music director takes a position in any church. Misunderstandings come about because of a lack in this area. This is not to say that everything must be put down in black and white, although that would not be wrong or out of place, but there should be a "gentlemen's agreement" or clear understanding of the exact duties and circumstances under which he must work. This can be taken care of in interviews prior to his coming.

Choosing a Part-time Music Director

1. *Finding a Candidate.* Most small churches are not financially able to hire a full-time director, or even a combination music and education director, or music and youth director. They may have to resort to hiring a member of the church as a part-time music director, or perhaps a student from a nearby college. The part-time music director does not have to be hired, but may be a volunteer from the congregation. Many good men in other pro-

fessions are good musicians and have been trained to some extent in this field. Although musical ability should be considered and given high priority, it is not the main consideration. The foremost prerequisite should be a dedicated Christian life and a desire to serve the church in a sincere manner. His loyalty to the pastor should be without question.

Desirable characteristics of a music director, full- or part-time, will be discussed in a later chapter.

2. *Making Sure of Ability.* Any person being considered for as part-time music director should be carefully scrutinized as to his musical ability. If the pastor is not adept or proficient in music himself, he should get counsel from reliable members of the church as to the abilities of a possible candidate. A personable, good, sincere man within the church who knows very little about music would not be a good candidate for the job of part-time music director. The prime qualification, beyond that of a sincere Christian attitude, is good musical ability.

3. *Providing Training and Encouragement.* Perhaps there are no men in the church with sufficient ability to qualify as part-time music directors. In this case, a likely candidate should be chosen and encouraged to spend time with the music director of a neighboring church or to take a course in the local university or college in conducting and song-leading. Pastors who have taken conducting and song leading in college can be of help to the man who has all the other qualifications but is lacking in musical training. A sincere Christian man who desires to help his church, is personable and has a good platform appearance, and is willing to spend time learning to direct music, would make a good part-time music director.

He should be taught many things, among them, (a) to use the rhythm patterns in directing songs (See page 196 for rhythm patterns and explanation.); (b) to announce the song numbers to the audience clearly and distinctly; (c) not to talk a great deal between stanzas or between songs; (d) how to sit on the platform, paying close attention during all the service; (e) how to direct the music for a large or small congregation (by this I mean he should be taught how to vary the size of the patterns that he uses, according to the size of the audience, and I will say more concerning this in the chapter on congregational singing and song leading); (f) to keep track of the songs used in each service so that he does not sing the same songs too often; (g) to follow the order of service correctly; (h) that the pastor is the leader of every service when present; (i) how to work with the accompanists; and (j) how to care for the musical instruments, making sure they are tuned periodically.

4. *Understanding of Policies and Duties.* Because many part-time music directors are part of the congregation prior to assuming their new duties, it is even more important that they understand the policies of the pastor and the church, and exactly what their duties will be, before taking the position. Many times a person who performs this task without charge to the church feels that he is entitled to a few liberties. It should be understood, in the beginning, that he is to follow the leadership of the pastor. This will prevent a great many problems in the future.

Counseling with the Music Director

1. *Frequency.* Because the music director and the pastor work so closely together in the services, the pastor should counsel with the music director frequently. The pastor should not give the music director specific orders, or make him feel that he has to discuss every little problem, but he should try to estabish a good rapport between them, so that, whenever the need arises, they may confer.

The pastor and the music director should get to know each other, perhaps on a little more intimate basis than the pastor and other staff members.

2. *Place.* The pastor's counseling should be done largely in private, whether in his office or in the music director's office. In any situation, no matter how close the pastor and his music director are in their personal lives, when each puts himself completely into his work, they will not see eye to eye in every situation. The

pastor, a leader of the church, at times will have to disagree with certain actions or policies of the music director. His disagreement should always be kept on the highest Christian plane, and be expressed in private. Occasionally, there might be a need for the pastor to reprimand the music director; this also should be done in private. Public reprimands are most embarrassing and actually cause the congregation to sympathize with the music director or other person being reprimanded, and to oppose the pastor, or the reprimander. Therefore, the wise pastor will do his correcting in private. This will cause the music director to be more appreciative of him, and will draw them together.

3. *Subject of Discussions.* The music director and pastor should discuss many aspects of the church work, but some are so important they should have priority. They should discuss the order of service, problems that occasionally arise in the service, how to properly sing the invitation song, and changes to be made from time to time in the services. At times the music director and the pastor should evaluate the music program, to see if it is supplying the musical needs of the church.

The Pastor of the Music Program

Every pastor should be the head or the pastor of every phase of the church program: the board of deacons, the board of trustees, the finances of the church, the youth program, the Sunday school, the missionry society, the Training Union, *and* the choir program. And because he is the pastor of the music program, there are certain duties to be performed by him and certain considerations given to him.

He Determines the Direction of the Music Program

As stated earlier, the pastor should be acutely aware of the needs of his people, not only in Bible teaching or preaching, but in the music program also. Every pastor should insist that the church have the kind of music program that he feels best for them.

He Guides in the Choosing of the Hymns

In each hymnal there are many songs not particularly good as congregational hymns. A relatively untrained part-time music director may not recognize exactly which hymns would make good congregational songs and which would not. Many times, too, the music director may differ with the pastor as to what type hymn should be sung in the services. The pastor should have some method of choosing what type hymns the congregation should sing. He could take the church hymnal and very carefully go through it, page by page, and mark the hymns he thinks best for the people to sing. He should give this book to the music director, asking him to choose songs from the ones marked. Of course, new songs can be added from time to time, and there are ways to do this, which will be discussed in a later chapter.

He Oversees Content and Preparation

Every music director will have a tendency to veer a little to the right or to the left of the music preference indicated by the pastor; therefore, it is up to the pastor to keep a close eye on the music program to make sure that the content is all that it should be at all times. He should also notice whether or not the music seems to be well prepared. This is one area in which he can be of great help to the music director, encouraging him to make sure that every number is well prepared before presenting it in the church services.

He Approves Special Singers

Every special singer that goes on the platform should be approved by the pastor. This is important for several reasons. First of all, the pastor would come nearer knowing the lives of the church members than would the music director. Because every person who sings on the platform—in a special group or as a soloist—should be exemplary in his Christian life, the pastor should determine who will or will not sing. This is for the protection of the services as well as for the protection of the music director. Any criticism that might come to the music director because of some special singer that he has chosen is then referred to the pastor. For example, John Doe is approved by the pastor to sing solos occasionally for the church services. One of the church members comes to the music director and says, "Did you know that John does such-and-such almost every week? Why do you have him singing solos? I don't think he should be singing solos before the congregation when his life is not what it ought to be." The music director, perhaps unaware of this, could then say to the church member, "The pastor approves all who sing in special groups or who sing solos on the platform; therefore, that should be taken up with the pastor." You can see how this would protect the music director.

He Determines the Order of Service

The pastor should determine when the congregation sings, when the Scriptures are read, when the offering is to be taken, and so on. He may make up the order of service and give a copy of it to the music director, who will then furnish a copy each week to everyone on the platform. But the original order should be determined by the pastor himself. This order of service could be followed each week. This is not to say that the pastor should not consult with the music director or other members of the staff in determining the order of service.

He Helps Promote the Music Program

Just as no other phase of the church program can be successful without active promotion by the pastor, the music program is destined to failure without his active promotion.

People will not join the choirs, as they ought to, unless they feel that the pastor is 100 percent in favor of the choir program. The pastor ought occasionally to talk to the congregation about the need for a good choir—their need to give their talents to the Lord and to serve him in this way. The pastor should occasionally brag on the choir and the fine job done by the music director. Most pastors desire to do this. This encourages the choir and helps them to know that the pastor is pleased. It makes for a much better spirit between the pastor and the music director. Many times, the difference between success and failure in the building of a good choir program would be the promotion, or lack of promotion, of the choir program by the pastor.

Musical events such as the Christmas cantata or the Easter musical program should be promoted from the pulpit by the pastor. These events will be very lightly attended if the people are not sure that the pastor is in favor of them or that he intends to be there himself and expects them to be there.

In summary, every pastor ought to become the "pastor" of the music program of his church. Pastors should keep a close eye on the music program, help the music director in the promotion, encourage him, counsel with him, and be a definite part of this phase of the work God has called them to do.

Bob Moore, Marietta (Georgia) Baptist Tabernacle, has some definite ideas on this subject, and has shared them with us.

THE PASTOR AND THE MUSIC DIRECTOR
by Bob Moore

It seems natural to write this article because I can simply draw on my feelings regarding a former music director, Lindsay Terry. What a sweet relationship we had, not only as pastor and music director, but also as friends.

Let me list five guiding principles which I regard as essential.

1. When you select a music director, select one whose professional abilities you can respect and whose loyalty you can trust. Most problems would be eliminated in the beginning by proper selection of a person to do the job. This does not mean your music director has to be a Lindsay Terry: there are not many of those available. But there are other men available with great potential.

Choose someone who has the background or training to do the job you need done.

2. Give the music director room to express his individuality and opportunity to have his own ministry. It is weak leadership, rather than strong, that does not allow another man to become master and leader of his own area of the work. If I were an authority on music, I perhaps would not need a music director. If I choose a man whom God has called for this work, I ought to supply him opportunity to develop his ministry. It is necessary that I not always have my mind made up ahead of time as to how to reach a desired effect. Of course, I hasten to say that as pastor I reserve the right to approve or disapprove anything in the music program, and I expect my music director to be flexible to my leadership.

3. Expect the music director to produce results, results that contribute to the total church program. Everyone is not a natural "go-getter." It follows that every time there is delegation of responsibility there must be examination of the results and evaluation. A good pastoral leader will be able to correct his music director in a proper way to benefit the program.

4. The music director is to have a heart for souls. Keep the thought ever before him that soul-winning is the most important activity in the world. Develop in him the philosophy that the singing should set the stage for winning souls. He should also be a soul-winner in his personal life.

5. Give praise. Honey draws flies much better than vinegar. If rebuke is needed, then it must be given: but usually if the person is the right kind of Christian worker, he will punish himself more than I could ever do. Praise builds self-confidence and produces better work.

4

The Music Director

EVERY part-time or full-time music director should feel definitely that he is in God's will in his present place of service. Few people in the church have as important a position as does the music director, other than the pastor. Because his position requires him to have such a large part in the public services, he should be God's choice for that particular job in the church which he serves.

Many people have the mistaken idea that a music director waves his arms on Sunday morning, leads the congregational singing, leads the choir, is in charge of a few specials, and his week's work is over. Nothing could be further from the truth, concerning the kind of music director every church should have. The short time spent in the Sunday services is only the showcase of many hours of work done during the week. All that a music director is and does comes together at this particular time. This is the time for which he has prepared all week. Whether he succeeds or fails depends upon the singers and musicians and his work through the week.

As has been stated earlier in this book, nothing is more needful

in churches today than God-called music directors. God needs
men who are willing to give of themselves in this important task.

A Full-time or Part-time Music Director

Many churches cannot afford to hire a full-time music director.
This does not in any way relieve the part-time or "volunteer"
music director from being all that he should be, in the sight of God
and of the church that he serves. The attitudes, insight, and characteristics of the full-time music director ought to be embodied in
a part-time music director.

More is expected of a full-time music director, because he is
paid to give his time to this task. Most part-time music directors
have other work to finance their living. Although music directors
have other tasks that do not pertain to the music program—visitation, teaching Sunday School, youth work, and perhaps correlat-
ing religious education—their foremost task is to see that the
church has the best music program possible. When guests visit a
home, the family members try to see that the room where the
guests will be entertained is even more immaculately kept than
other parts of the home. The public services are the "living rooms"
of the church, where people come to enjoy the church. This is
where they spend their time and where they should feel welcome.
This is where they should see the church operating at its maximum efficiency. Because this is true, the music director should be
enthusiastic about having the kind of music program that will
cause visitors and members to go away saying, "It was good to be
in the house of the Lord today," or cause those without Christ
to be led to a knowledge of him, partly because of an evangelistic music program.

Naturally the part-time music director is not expected to spend
as much time as a full-time man but if he assumes the responsibility of the music program of his church, then he should see to it
that his church has as good a music program as he can cause to
come into being. Anything less than this, even from a part-time
music director, is sinful in the sight of God. Bear in mind, however,

that God does not expect more than a man has. He does not expect one to give of talents he does not possess, but he does say, "It is required in stewards that a man be found faithful." Either a part-time or full-time music director should be sure to give his best.

Attitude

The attitude of the music director is of prime importance. Many talented music directors have had their programs curtailed by their bad attitudes. If the music director's attitude is unbecoming to a dedicated Christian, it would indicate that perhaps he is not in the position that God would have him in, or that his heart is not right toward the work God has given him to do.

The attitude of the music director should be right as concerns the following:

The Church Member

Every music director should keep in mind that he is to be a servant of the church. Too many music directors are willing and ready to receive with open arms the generosities of the church members, but they are not willing to reciprocate. Let it also be kept in mind that the church members pay the salary of the music director. They have the right to expect of him a certain amount of his time, energy, and effort.

Every music director should spend time in prayer, asking God to give him a good attitude toward the members of his church. This is very difficult in the face of criticism or shortsightedness on the part of people, but it is one of the difficult tasks of being a music director. A good attitude pays off in large dividends. Music directors should learn to love people; people will return his love.

The Music Program

The music program is the task to which God has called the music director and should receive his primary attention. He should determine that, under God, he will develop the best possible music program for his church. Many directors could have a much better music program if they spent a little more time and effort in consciously trying to make it the best possible.

No aspect of the music program is of little importance. Anything worth doing at all is worth doing well. If a music director trains a quartet, then it should be the best quartet that can be developed in the church. Every aspect of the program should strive to be the best part of the music program.

Thousands of people have been attracted to a particular church because of an excellent music program; therefore, no part of the work of any church should surpass her music program.

The Pastor

Above all, the music director should realize that the thirteenth chapter of Hebrews applies to him also. Any time God chose to lead a group of people he did so by using one man. God usually spoke to this individual, and he to the people. The same is true today. When God leads a church to become a great lighthouse—a great soul-winning station—he uses an individual. The pastor should oversee the whole church; the music director must recognize him as overseer. He may not always agree with the pastor, but his wishes and desires must be subordinate to the wishes and desires of the pastor.

Many people consider the music director as "second fiddle" to the pastor. Humanly speaking, this is true in every sense of the word. Although God does not have any second, third, fourth, or first fiddles, every man who does the will of God and tries his best to please him, plays first fiddle as far as God is concerned.

Blessed is the music director who keeps in focus his position in respect to the pastor. Never should a day go by but that the music director prays for the pastor, asking God to direct him in every activity. He should feel free to communicate with the pastor on any subject, and should provide the pastor with plenty of time to counsel with him. His good attitude toward the pastor in everyday life, all week long, will make for a good attitude on the platform during the public services.

His Helpers

No music director can carry on a full music program without help from other people; therefore, his attitude toward those who help him should be one of kindness and appreciation. Perhaps he knows more about the music program or about music in general than they do, but his appreciative attitude toward them will cause them to do a much better job, even in their limited capacity. Never should he give the impression (*in any way*) that he is better than they; that attitude would only ostracize him.

Choir Members

A music director's attitude should be the finest toward the members of his choirs. His choirs are made up of individuals who have feelings and personalities that must be considered. Each person likes to have a certain amount of credit when a performance has been particularly good. Each wants to be recognized by the director for what he is and who he is. If a music director can establish good rapport between himself and his choir members, then 90 per cent of his battles are over. The music will be sweeter, the attitude of the choir will be better, and the services will benefit from the closeness of the music director and choir members.

The director should lead the choir members to understand that his position carries with it a certain authority in rehearsals and in the music activities under his direction. He must, at all times, command the respect of those who sing under him. This he can do only if they see that he means business and attempts to be fair with them in all things. They must know first, though, that he loves them.

The Accompanists

The pianist and the organist can do much to make a music director look good. It has almost become my conviction that no music program can far exceed the ability of the accompanists. There are ways to compensate for the lack of ability on the part of the accompanists. When possible, it should be done; but, as a general rule the music chain cannot be stronger than this particular link.

Just as the pastor and the music director should have a good attitude toward each other, the music director and the accompanists should have a good working relationship, mainly because they work so closely together in the public services. Never be mistaken about this fact: the audience can tell when there is enmity between the music director and his accompanists. Such attitudes grieve the Holy Spirit and will, in many cases, hinder the public services.

Here again, the music director must let it be known that he is in charge and has responsibilities and authority under the general leadership of the pastor. Once the accompanists understand this, a certain amount of rapport is built up automatically. Every music director should strive for as good a working relationship as possible between himself and the accompanists.

Training

While every full-time music director is expected to have adequate training for his position, many part-time music directors have had little or no formal training. The full-time music director should never be content with past successes; he should be always looking for new ideas and new ways of developing his music program. His training or learning should never end; when it does, his effectiveness ends. It is good for a music director to attend summer music camps or seminars. Several good seminars are held each year throughout the United States. Many churches will pay the expenses of their music directors to these. Just as a doctor needs to keep abreast of the changing practices in the medical world, a music director needs to keep abreast of new developments, new music, and new techniques. It is easy for music directors to slip into complacency, while their methods could be greatly improved and augmented by a week in a good music seminar, getting new ideas for conducting and directing.

The part-time music director should also take every opportunity to learn to do his job better. If he is near a college or university (preferably a Christian college), he should audit classes in conducting, song leading, and music theory. If he is not paid by the church, the church should bear the expense of his classroom activities. If this is not possible, he should contact a full-time music director in whom he has confidence, and seek advice and counsel. Usually, a full-time music director with formal training, whose aid is sought by one who wants to become a better part-time music director, will help in every way possible.

Weekly sessions should be arranged, for the trained musician to teach the untrained how to direct a choir, to lead the congregational singing, to announce the numbers, to recuit new choir members, and to develop small groups and ensembles. Every pastor who has a part-time music director should see to it that he has some kind of training to qualify him to direct the music of the church. The pastor can help by teaching him how to sit on the platform, how to announce the numbers, what to say and what not to say between numbers, and how to approach the pulpit. Hundreds of services have been ruined because a pastor did not have the foresight or take the time to go over a few details with the untrained music director, to make the services more enjoyable. It is not a disgrace for a church to have a part-time music director with no training, but this situation should not continue without effort toward improvement.

Insight

Every music director should realize that God has given him a job to do, and should look for ways to do it better. He should ask God to give him more ability to meet the real spiritual needs of the people, through the music program. He should make notes often when confronted with a situation over which he has no control so that he might improve the situation should it occur at a later time.

Soul-Winning

Any music director can do a much better job on Sunday if he has spent some time during the week in witnessing, trying to win people to Jesus Christ. He should have a fire burning within his heart on Sunday during the services, and there is no better way to kindle it than through soul-winning. This will cause the services to be more enjoyable to him, and will cause him to do a better job.

The music director should set a definite time each week to go soul-winning; if this is not done, he usually will not go as he should. A soul-winning music director communicates his feelings and the burden on his heart more effectively. Just as the pastor, the Sunday school teachers, the associate pastors and others of the church are expected to win souls and to witness for Jesus Christ, it is the director's duty to do the same.

Personal Characteristics

A music director should be honest, upright, amiable, loving, kind, happy, respectful, cheerful, and determined. He should not necessarily possess all these qualities at one and the same time, but they should be, eventually a part of his make-up. These are positive aspects.

Now consider a few negative ones. May God have mercy on a *lazy* music director. Many good directors receive a certain amount of reproach because of lazy predecessors. There is no place in the field of music for a lazy person. A music director should check the list and see if he has the desirable characteristics and leaves off the undesirable. If not, he should make every effort to acquire as many desirable characteristics as possible.

Charisma

The word "charisma" has come to mean something altogether different from what is here intended. No reference to the Pentecostal use of the term is meant, but rather the leadership ability of the music director to relate to the audience and to instill within them a desire to sing and participate in the service, following his directions. Every director does not have this innately, but should strive for a better director-audience relationship. Often different geographical locations affect this, but a wise director will have character enough to say to himself, "I'll do whatever is necessary, short of compromising my convictions, to lead these people in the way that will honor Christ." A good audience-director relationship is sometimes long in coming but the sweetness of the accomplishment always mellows the experience in reaching the desired goal.

One of the best ways for an aspiring young music director to develop charisma with an audience is to watch carefully some outstanding directors, noting procedures, mannerisms and methods they use in "reaching" an audience. He should not become a carbon copy, but he should try to gain from these directors some tips to help him improve. Then, too, on occasion, he can learn how not to reach an audience by carefully observing a music director lose contact with the people.

Cultivating leadership ability is another effort to reach people with the gospel of Jesus Christ. Many would say that the Holy Spirit can override human failures and weaknesses, but God gives us knowledge and ability and expects us to be "as wise as serpents and harmless as doves." He expects us to "pray as if everything depended on Him and work as if everything depended on us." He expects us to approach every service as though it were our last one and to strive with everything that is in us to reach every last person in the audience. Sometimes it is only done through the music and the music director.

In summary, a music director, full-time or part-time, should make sure he is the best music director that he can be. Make sure that his attitudes, training, insight, soul-winning, and personal characteristics are all that they can be under God.

5

Discovering Prospects

"WHAT is the music potential of my church?" The answer to this question is important for every music director to know, and there *are* ways to find out. A churchwide music survey is the best way to determine exactly the music potential in the church. Consider five things concerning this music survey.

What the Survey Contains

On the following page is a copy of the music survey blank used annually at the First Baptist Church of Hammond, Indiana. It asks for enough information concerning each person who fills out one to help any music director determine the music potential of his church. The information asked for in the first section is of vital importance. Parents of Primary or Beginner children should fill out a survey form for them.

Why a Survey Should Be Taken

First, it answers the inevitable question, "Who can I get to sing in the choir?" In five minutes on Sunday morning, the answers can be determined. Second, the survey also shows the musical training and the background of prospects.

How to Take the Music Survey

Discuss It with the Pastor

Before taking a music survey discuss it with the pastor. After getting his approval, the music director and the pastor should determine the date for the survey and the procedure to be used.

Discuss It with the Teachers and Officers of the Sunday School

At First Baptist Church, Hammond, Indiana, and at other churches the writer has served, the pastor, at the regular teachers' and officers' meeting, discusses the intent to take the churchwide survey the next Sunday. Each person is given a music survey blank so that he may become familiar with it, and be able to explain it to his pupils.

The teachers and officers are told of the tremendous importance of the survey to the music program of the church and are asked to get a blank filled out by every person in their departments or classes. Those presently in the choir should also fill out survey blanks because of the importance of answers providing other than choir information.

Take the Survey During Sunday School

The superintendents and teachers take the survey blanks with them to the classes or departments on the next Sunday morning, and take about five minutes to have each pupil fill out the blanks and turn them in. When the survey blanks are handed in with the regular Sunday school records, they are given to the music director.

Music Survey

"Let the word of Christ dwell in you richly in all wisdom; teaching admonishing one another in psalms and hymns and spiritual songs, singing with grace in your hearts to the Lord" (Col. 3:16).

NAME _____ BIRTH DATE _____ ADULT _____

ADDRESS _____ CITY _____ STATE _____ PHONE _____

ARE YOU A CHRISTIAN? _____ CHURCH MEMBER? _____ WHERE? ___

TO WHICH SUNDAY SCHOOL CLASS OR DEPARTMENT DO YOU BELONG? _____

* * *

ARE YOU PRESENTLY SINGING IN A CHOIR OF THE CHURCH? _____

WOULD YOU BE INTERESTED IN SINGING IN ONE OF THE CHOIRS OF THE CHURCH? _____

HAVE YOU BEEN IN A CHOIR BEFORE? _____ WHERE? _____

CHECK YOUR VOICE RANGE: HIGH VOICE _____ LOW VOICE _____

DO YOU PLAY A MUSICAL INSTRUMENT? _____ NAME THE INSTRUMENT _____

HAVE YOU EVER LED SINGING? _____

HAVE YOU HAD ANY TYPE OF MUSICAL TRAINING? _____

WHAT TYPE? _____ HOW LONG? _____

* * *

CHECK GROUP TO WHICH YOU WOULD BELONG

ADULT ___ TEENS ___ JUNIOR ___ PRIMARY ___ BEGINNER ___

(18–up)   (13–17)   (9–12)   (6–8)   (4–5)

*   PARENTS SIGN FOR PRIMARIES AND BEGINNERS

– REMARKS –

_____

_____

_____

_____

I WILL NOT BE ABLE TO BE A REGULAR CHOIR MEMBER BUT I WOULD LIKE TO KNOW MORE ABOUT THE SUBSTITUTE PLAN _____

I POSSIBLY COULD BE A SUBSTITUTE _____

How to Break Down the Music Survey

The music director should go through the survey blanks and divide them by departments, then separate them into two categories: (1) Choir prospects and (2) non-prospects. The names of the choir prospects should be given to the directors of each choir. (Many music directors have other persons working with them as directors of the different choirs and helpers in other music activities.)

Other Uses of the Survey

The first section of the survey blanks may reveal some church prospects. Also, there may be found some who have had experience in song leading. Perhaps some can play the piano or other instruments; some have had voice training. This information will be useful in gradually building a great music program.

6

Preparing Music for Rehearsals

SOME of the most valuable time in any music program is the time spent in preparing the music and preparing for rehearsal time. The choir or any special group can tell if the music director is ill prepared. Time spent in preparation insures against a faltering, slipshod, weak music program. Inadequate preparation leads to frequent repetition of special numbers in the services. This does not mean repeating some special arrangements is not warranted. But to repeat because of lack of preparation is shirking one's duty.

Making Your Own Arrangements

Many music directors, especially those with some knowledge of the piano keyboard, could put a great deal more life and enthusiasm in their music program if they did some of their own arranging.

Experiment by taking a simple hymn and changing it slightly. Put in modulations, special introductions, or special closings to make it sound new and different. By paying close attention to

Hallelujah, What A Saviour

published arrangements one can gather ideas of how to do arrangements for his own choir. Music directors who do not have a knowledge of the keyboard may have good ideas and may obtain help from a pianist or organist in putting on paper his particular arrangements. Often a choir will take pride in doing an arrangement, however simple, written by their "very own" choir director.

Occasionally a special type song is needed and a proper arrangement cannot be found in published work. This should give a director the motivation to try his hand at arranging.

The illustration on page 48 is a simple arrangement of "Hallelujah, What A Saviour" that can be done by any choir. It can be effective for a special service on the cross or at Easter time.

Pages 50–52 present an arrangement of "All Hail the Power of Jesus' Name." This is a combination of three different melodies using the same lyrics by Edward Perronet.

Both of these arrangements are thrilling when done effectively and with a measure of skill. Neither is difficult, either in arrangement or in ability required to perform them.

In looking for arrangements for your choir several things should be kept in mind.

The Degree of Difficulty

Many choirs are well trained and able to do difficult choir arrangements; they have a broader scope to choose from. Fewer arrangements are currently being published for lesser-trained choirs. One fault of publishing companies is that they make choir arrangements too difficult for 90 percent of the volunteer church choirs. The John T. Benson Publishing Company, in Nashville, Tennessee, is publishing more and more for the lesser-trained choirs, while still providing a challenging grade of arrangements. This seems to be, since they published a book of my choir arrangements entitled *Sing of Him,* intended for the average volunteer church choir.

All Hail The Power Of Jesus' Name

E. Perronet

Oliver Holden
Arr. by Lindsay Terry

FULL CHOIR
Rapidly

All hail the power of Je - sus' name, let an - gels pros-trate fall. Bring forth the roy - al di – a - dem and crown Him Lord of＿ all. Bring forth the roy - al di – a - dem and crown Him Lord ＿ of all.

(Perronet - Wm. Shrubsole)
MEN - Unison

Let ev - 'ry kin - dred, ev – 'ry tribe on this ter - res trial ball,

LADIES - Unison

FULL CHOIR

To Him all maj - es - ty as – cribe and crown Him, crown Him,

(Perronet - James Ellor)

crown Him! O that with yon - der sa - cred throng, we

crown Him! O that with yon - der sa - cred throng, we

crown Him! O that with yon - der sa - cred throng, we

crown Him! O that with yon - der sa - cred throng,

at His feet may fall we at His feet may fall; We'll join the ev - er -

at His feet may fall, we at His feet may fall; We'll join the ev - er -

at His feet may fall, we at His feet may fall; We'll join the ev - er -

we at His feet may fall; We'll join the ev - er -

Evangelistic Scope

In choosing a piece of music, the director should give priority to the message of the choir arrangements, after the degree of difficulty has been determined. Today many petty, shallow songs are being written that are not suitable for an evangelistic service, because they have no real biblical message. They should be avoided for use in regular church services.

The Places to Search

A choir director for seventeen years, I have searched in a multitude of places for good choir arrangements. Whenever you find some, latch onto them. Make notes on where to obtain copies; keep a file on these prospective choir arrangements. This writer lets many songleaders and choir directors go through his files and glean from them choir arrangements that they can use. Others allow him to do the same in their offices and files. Finding fresh, new material is a never-ending job. It keeps a choir director fresh year after year. A choir director should never be too proud to ask other directors—even directors with smaller choirs than his—to send him sample arrangements. Every choir director has some good choir arrangement or idea that you do not have; therefore, glean from as many as possible.

A choir director should never overlook the advertisements for choir arrangements that come to his mailbox or the church, some simply addressed to "Music Director." These may come as second- or third-class mail but may still be a lead to at least one good choir arrangement. Often only one suitable choir arrangement can be found in a whole book of arrangements.

Learning the Music

Fortunate is the director who can play the piano well enough to sit down and play through new arrangements and learn them. But

Never Alone

Anonymous

Arr. Lindsay Terry

INTRO.

Nev - er a - lone, Nev - er a - lone, Nev - er a - lone.

A

How man - y times dis - cour - aged, We sink be - side the way; A -

bout us all is dark - ness, we hard - ly dare to pray. Then from the

mists and shad - ows, the sweet - est voice e'er known says, "Child, am I not

any director without this ability should schedule time with his accompanist to learn the new arrangements before he introduces them to the choir. Not that the director should memorize the music, but he should be familiar with all of the key changes, the passages that may require some "woodshedding," and any special introductions, closings, or codas.

The choir will gain confidence if they sense that the conductor has spent time preparing for the rehearsal by learning the numbers so he can teach them. With added respect for the conductor, the choir members will be more prompt in their attendance and more faithful in rehearsals and performances.

Certain passages will need to be rehearsed in sections. This should be anticipated before the rehearsal time and the individual parts learned so that sectional rehearsals can be carried on with confidence. The following is an example of an arrangement that is simple, but has several difficult passages that may need sectional rehearsing.

Keeping Ahead of the Schedule

A special calendar should be maintained by the music director so that he can determine, three or four weeks in advance, exactly what special numbers he will use in the services. These should be planned far ahead of schedule. In most cases a choir director should know several days in advance what arrangements he will work on and what music he needs to have ready for the services ahead. The following is a schedule or format of a choir rehearsal period used by the writer.

A new choir director can have a much more effective music program if plans are made, in detail, far enough in advance so that musicians and singers might be working diligently toward a particular service. This is one advantage in having several people involved in the music program, and several ensembles, duets, or soloists participating in addition to the graded choirs.

CHOIR REHEARSAL

_____

Cong. Songs _____

_____

_____

_____

Prayer

Next Special _____

Next Opening _____

Coming Specials _____

_____   _____

_____   _____

Other Activities:

Offering

Announcements _____

_____

_____

MUSIC INSTRUCTION

MUSIC PUBLISHERS

The following is a list of publishers who can supply good evangelistic arrangements, and arrangements for duets, trios, and quartets.

Singspiration, Inc.
Zondervan Publishing House
Grand Rapids, Michigan

The Rodeheaver, Hall-Mack Company
Winona Lake,
Indiana

Gospel Publishing House
Springfield,
Missouri

Broadman Press
Nashville,
Tennessee

John T. Benson Publishing Company
Nashville,
Tennessee

Lillenas Publishing Company
Kansas City,
Missouri

7

The Adult Choir

THE adult or senior choir is the best and most widely used in most churches; therefore, consideration should be given to this choir first. Nine points of consideration are listed.

Rebuilding an Existing Choir

Most churches, however large or small, have some kind of an adult choir that is used in at least one service on Sunday. Perhaps, for some reason, this choir should be rebuilt. The music survey may provide prospects for rebuilding an existing choir.

First of all, the existing choir should be surveyed to determine its strong and weak points. Begin reorganizing as though a brand new choir were being formed. Recruit as many new members as possible, as soon as possible. Set down choir rules and regulations and let the choir know these will be kept. In general, the choir should understand that they are passing into a new era, and things will be done differently henceforth. This action must be taken in Christian love, with much diplomacy.

Many of the following suggestions about building a new choir may also be used in rebuilding an existing choir.

Starting a New Choir

Set a meeting time when as many prospective choir members as possible can come. Contact prospects whose name and phone numbers are on the survey blanks. A good accompanist, and acceptable rehearsal time should have already been chosen.

The first meeting gives opportunity for the director to set down the rules and regulations and map out future plans for the choir. The director should convey his own real enthusiasm about this ministry.

The Weekly Rehearsal

1. *Start and stop on time.*   The choir will appreciate this consideration and attention to punctuality. People in the jet age are busy. If they know they will be able to start practicing at a given time and stop at a set time, they will not hesitate to set aside this time for practice. Keep their confidence by keeping your starting and stopping time rigid.

2. *Use several selections at each rehearsal.*   Start rehearsals or practice times, whichever you prefer to call them, by singing through each hymn for the following Sunday's congregational singing. Spend the next fifteen to twenty minutes on the choir arrangement for the next Sunday's services. Then go from song to song, using four to six songs in each rehearsal, spending about ten minutes on each. There are two reasons for using several selections. First, it breaks the monotony; perhaps more important, it allows them to practice a song at four or five rehearsals. This is much more important than spending an hour and a half or two hours on one or two arrangements. If a choir member has to miss rehearsal, he has already practiced the song in three or four other rehearsals; therefore he should be able to perform consistently with the choir. Close rehearsal by repeating next Sunday's arrangement.

3. *Have a few breaks in the practice time.* Do not sing a choir hard for extended periods, particularly when working with untrained voices. They need a rest, or "breather," occasionally.

4. *Prepare the accompanists ahead of time.* Don't embarrass the accompanists by putting new music in front of them and expecting them to play it the first time they see it. They will appreciate a chance to go over it in privacy a few times before coming to the choir rehearsal.

5. *Don't be too serious all through the rehearsal.* Be light and jovial. That is not to say that the director should try to be a clown, but he should try to be lighthearted once in awhile, letting the singers relax.

6. *Demand Discipline.* Without being a tyrant, command and demand strict choir discipline. You cannot get the allotted work done in rehearsal without good discipline.

7. *Choose a good place to practice.* Many choirs, by necessity, have to practice in the choir loft in which they will be performing. This can be a drawback, because of the largeness of the room. If possible, go to another room which gives good sound for hearing all the parts. Choose a well-ventilated, light, cheerful room. Make sure you have good instruments. Perhaps rehearsal may be ended by singing Sunday's song in the choir loft.

8. *The choir director should keep ahead of his choir.* Keep ahead musically, by knowing the arrangements in advance of rehearsal. Keep ahead by having plenty of music for them to work on at each rehearsal. A well-planned rehearsal assures confidence on the part of the director. If his morale is high, he can convey to the choir a high spirit of enthusiasm.

Sources of Material

Several companies can supply good evangelistic choir arrangements. Their musicians take a simple hymn or gospel song and change it into a beautiful, challenging choir song. Following is a list of several such companies and their addresses.

MUSIC PUBLISHERS

Evangelistic choir arrangements can be secured from the following companies:

1. Singspiration, Inc.
   Zondervan Publishing House
   Grand Rapids, Mich.

2. John T. Benson Publishing Company
   1625 Broadway Street
   Nashville, Tenn.

3. Manna Music Inc.
   1328 N. Highland Ave.
   Hollywood, Calif.   90028

4. Mosie Lister Publications
   Tampa, Fla.

5. The Rodeheaver, Hall-Mack Company
   Winona Lake, Ind.

6. Gospel Publishing House
   Springfield, Mo.

7. Lillenas Publishing Company
   Kansas City, Mo.

8. Broadman Press
   Nashville, Tenn.

9. Accent, Inc.
   Box 37, Station C,
   Grand Rapids, Mich.   49506

Keeping Contact with the Members

Any good choir director will keep up with his choir members. Have the choir secretary check the roll at each rehearsal. If a choir member is not present, find out why. Ask the choir members to call if they cannot be present for a rehearsal. Periodic choir letters to all participants encourages faithfulness. Absentee letters will keep nonattendance at a minimum.

Recruiting New Members

As new members join the church, find out if they would like to sing in the choir. Keep working on the prospects received from the survey; contact and enlist them, if possible. A choir grows in the same way as a Sunday school class—by personal contact.

Motiviating Faithfulness

Regularly stress faithfulness. Remind the members that every choir is made up of individuals; if individuals are not present, the choir is not present. Help them realize that it is just as important for them to be in place as for the choir director to be in his place. God rewards faithfulness. Place the choir on a very high plane. Guide them to see that this is *their* place of service, and that it is a *very important* place of service.

Music Training

Presented near the close of this book, pages 191 through 198, are the materials the author uses in training his choirs in the fundamentals of music. A few moments during each of several choir rehearsals may be used to teach some of these facts and skills, or you may call attention to certain music fundamentals at rehearsals each week. Either way, strive to help all members attain knowledge of the fundamentals of music; they will be better choir members.

8

The Teenage Choir

SPECIAL attention has been drawn to my music ministry, in which I have been able, with God's help, to build three large teenage choirs. Some people find this almost unbelievable today. I contend that teenagers are the same in this day as in every other. Of course, they have different motivations, different environments, but basically they are the same.

In building teenage choirs we use essentially the same system as with an adult choir; yet it is quite different in some ways, because teens are involved.

Starting a New Choir

It is best not to rebuild an existing choir, but to dissolve it and start anew.

1. *Set a meeting time.* Set the time at three or four weeks ahead. Go to every teenage department of the Sunday school telling them of your plans to build a large teenage choir, letting them know the date of the first meeting. Make sure they know

that this is not a practice time; it is a meeting with those interested in filling out applications to become members of a teenage choir.

Announce that every person desiring membership in the new choir must fill out an application blank; the applications will be processed and all applicants will be notified as to whether or not they are accepted as members in the new choir. Talk it up big; make them realize that this is one of the most important teenage functions in the church, because it is.

When the day arrives for this first meeting do not be alarmed if you do not have a large crowd present; you will have, by the time several months have gone by. Just make sure, prior to the meeting, to build it up and boost it in every way possible.

2. *Give out the applications at the first meeting,* asking teens to take them home and prayerfully fill them out. The application is divided into three parts. The first part has primarily the same information on it as the church music survey. The second, and perhaps the most important part, is this: "State briefly your reasons for wanting to be a member of the Teen Choraliers." The reason must be a Christian one. The director must determine if the teenagers' motives are right, if they really want to be in the choir for spiritual reasons or just because the gang is there. Of course, some will be motivated for that reason, but at least they know they are supposed to be there for spiritual reasons. If an application comes back without a spiritual reason stated, it should be rejected and returned to the teenager with the tactful explanation that his reason must be Christian, since choir is a service for Christ.

3. *Consider the seven rules* in the last part of the application. The rules are these:

a. I will strive to be on time for every rehearsal.

b. I will strive to keep my mind on the business at hand during rehearsal as well as during the services.

c. I'll help to preserve the present conditions of all materials used, books, hymnals, and sheet music.

d. I will refrain from unnecessary talking during all rehearsals.

e. I will recognize the authority of the conductor in all matters pertaining to the choir.

f. Realizing that unnecessary activity in the choir during the church services distracts the attention of the audience, I will refrain from writing notes, chewing gum, thumbing through hymnals and being generally inattentive.

g. I will strive to be present for every rehearsal and performance.

The application is closed with this: "Having carefully read the above regulations, I prayerfully affix my signature." There is a place for the signature and the phone number. The phone number is of vital importance as the chief medium of contact.

4. *Receive the completed applications* at a meeting held about a week after they were taken home and filled out. At this time, map out plans for the choir. Let them know what is expected of them, and just exactly what they can expect from the director. Tell them exactly in what services they will sing. Share recreational or outing plans. Tell about the contests being planned.

5. *Choose a good name for the choir,* one that teenagers can be proud of. While I was music director of the Salem Baptist Church in Winston-Salem, North Carolina, the teenage choir was called the *Choral Teens.*

The teen choir should be the service choir for one service during the week, if possible—perhaps on Sunday evening or Wednesday evening. In Miami, Florida, at the Northwest Baptist Church, the teen choir was the Sunday morning service choir. In Winston-Salem, the teen choir was the Sunday evening choir; and at the First Baptist Church in Hammond, Indiana, the Teen Choraliers were the Wednesday evening choir.

6. *Place the choir on a high plane.* Make sure the teens know the seriousness of building a good choir, and that they are expected to work hard to make the choir something of which they can be proud, something that will bring honor to Christ and to the church.

Here is the application blank for membership in the Teen Choraliers of the First Baptist Church, Hammond, Indiana.

TEEN CHORALIERS
APPLICATION BLANK

NAME _____ AGE _____ BIRTH DATE Mo. ___ Day ___ Yr. ___

ADDRESS _____ CITY _____ SCHOOL _____

Are you a Christian? _____ Are you a church member? _____
Where? _____

Are you a member of the Sunday School? _____ What Dept.? _____

Teacher? _____

Do you have a low _____ or high _____ voice?

Have you had voice training? _____ Do you play an instrument? _____

Name the instrument _____ Have you been a member of a choir
before? _____

Where? _____ Name the choir(s) _____

State briefly your reasons for wanting to be a member of the "Teen
Choraliers."

_____
_____
_____
_____

The Bible teaches that all things done for Christ should be done decently and in order; therefore, the following rules and regulations have been instituted: As a member of the "Teen Choraliers," I will:

1. Strive to be on time for every rehearsal.
2. Strive to keep my mind on the business at hand during rehearsals as well as during the services.
3. Help to preserve the present condition of all materials used—books, hymnals, sheet music, etc.
4. Refrain from unnecessary talking during all rehearsals.
5. Recognize the authority of the conductor in all matters pertaining to the choir.
6. Realize that unnecessary activities in the choir during the church services distract the audience; therefore, I will refrain from writing notes, chewing gum, thumbing through hymnals, and being generally inattentive.
7. Strive to be present for every rehearsal and performance.

Having carefully read the above regulations, I prayerfully affix my signature.

_____

PHONE NUMBER _____

Teen Choraliers of Northwest Baptist Church, Miami, Florida. Enlisted and directed by Lindsay Terry, pictured in front of the choir.

Choir Practice Time

Always keep the rehearsals moving. Begin with prayer and go right into some lively song the group knows, to get their voices warmed up and to get their attention. Use several selections in each practice session, with several three-minute breaks to let the singers talk and relax a little. During this time the director can have opportunity to talk with the accompanist. Do not let breaks get out of hand; but, rather, make sure that, at the end of the break, the choir gets back to business.

Be very, very businesslike in dealings with the teenagers during rehearsals. In recreational times, be one of them; love them, let them know that you can be young and that you want to be one of them. But in rehearsal, be businesslike, conveying to them the message that you are quite serious about the task at hand.

The Kind of Music

Music should be evangelistic, but music used with the teenage choir should differ slightly from music used with the adult choir. It should be very solid and heartwarming. Use some three-part harmony arrangements—sopranos and altos and a third part for the boys, a baritone part. Neither tenor nor bass, that part is not too high or too low for young changing voices, which are seldom either a low teenage bass or a very high tenor. Many music publishers produce teenage choir arrangements in three-part harmony, called SAB, soprano, alto and baritone. The teens like to use music with life and challenge in it, songs of Christian testimony, and songs that present the love of Christ. Have something new and fresh for them to work on at each rehearsal.

Discipline

The first rehearsal sets the pace for discipline. From the very beginning, let every teen know that, when the director comes into the rehearsal room, he runs the show. He is the boss; they must do what he says. Of course he must love them, and they must know that he does. They must realize that following his leadership is the only way the rehearsal can be successful and honor Christ.

When they do exceptionally well, compliment them. When the choir has a good rehearsal, let them know it was. If they do an excellent job in a service, make some public mention of it. Make them act as they ought. In this day and time teenagers find a great deal of security in being made to do right. They are seldom disciplined at home or at school; if at choir rehearsal they are made to do right, they feel security and a sense of belonging. Underneath definite authority, show a great deal of love. Teens must realize their interest and the work of Christ is near the director's heart.

Keep in Contact with the Members

Keep an accurate account of attendance at each rehearsal and use the phone and personal contacts to keep up with absentees. Remind them that they promised to be present for every rehearsal and performance. While this is not to be held over their heads, they are to realize at all times that they are bound by their application pledge.

Recruiting New Members

Be on the alert for teenagers in the church who need to be in the choir. An annual music survey will help discover prospects.

Provide Outside Singing Opportunities

Other churches have revival meetings and might be delighted to have a teenage choir to come one night to sing for them. Perhaps the teens can sing for a conference or youth rally. Outside singing opportunities provide an outlet other than the regular services, in which they can be of service to Christ.

A sharply dressed youth ensemble from Chattanooga, Tennessee.

A teen ensemble from Marietta, Georgia on tour in the Bahama Islands.

Motivate Faithfulness

Try in the choir to instill a sense of faithfulness. This will help a great deal when they become adult choir members. Stress faithfulness often.

Train The Choir Musically

Take time in rehearsal to share the basic fundamentals of music. The public school system helps a great deal in this, but not all teens receive musical instruction in school.

Provide Some Recreation for Choir Members

This is especially needful if no other youth activities are provided by the church.

9

Children's Choirs

THE children should be divided into choirs according to grades. There are several reasons for having children's choirs. Many Primaries and Juniors are Christians and need a place of service to which they can give themselves and know they are serving Christ. There is something fresh and precious about a children's choir that adds greatly to the services. At the church where the writer serves, children's choirs take turns singing every third Wednesday night. They can be also used effectively in special Christmas, Thanksgiving, or Easter music programs.

Starting the Choirs

In starting the children's choirs, start big and recruit as rapidly as possible. At the first meetings make big plans. Juniors, Primaries, and Beginners like to be a part of the mass. Do not set the age limits too closely. Keep the age limits wide so that a maximum number of children may be in each choir. Have not less than three children's choirs, for the groups mentioned above. Since they are usually divided in that manner in Sunday school, they will resent any overlapping of the age span in the choirs. Juniors feel that they are much "bigger" than Primaries, and Primaries feel that Beginners are "babies"; therefore, it is better to separate them.

A good workable number for a Junior choir is fifty, while forty is about the maximum for Primaries. Twenty-five is tops for Beginners. When the choirs exceed these numbers, they should be divided. In Primary and Junior choirs separate boys and girls, when dividing, rather than ages. Juniors need an age span from the third to the sixth grade. The third and fourth graders give the volume needed, and the fifth and sixth graders lend a little more maturity and music knowledge to the group. Older juniors can sing parts readily.

People who have good rapport with children—and a keen imagination—should be used as directors for these choirs. Musical knowledge is just one qualification for the children's choir director. Their total qualifications should be considered carefully.

The church music director should keep in touch with younger choirs, making sure that they have needed materials and equipment, and proper space. He should help promote their attendance.

Each children's choir rehearsal should have a director and a pianist, plus two to three adult helpers, who will assist by (1) checking the roll; (2) helping to keep order; (3) getting the children ready to sing in a service; (4) canning and assisting at social events and parties; (5) transportation, and (6) passing out and collecting music sheets and books during rehearsals.

Music to Use

With Beginners use songs understood by and written for young children. They will sing meaningfully what is on their level. Primary and Junior choirs can use song arrangements, and will take pride in doing them well. Even some Primaries carry the alto part well. Do not be content with singing only choruses, but use *choir arrangements*. Several music publishers can supply these for children's choirs, and will send catalogs and/or samples upon request.

Make sure the children learn their parts correctly. They should not merely sing words but should be taught the meaning of the lyrics they sing. Help them to understand that they are to convey to the audience a message in song. Remember, many of them have already become Christians.

Social Acitivites

Have occasional parties or social activities with the children's choirs, but let these things work for you. Let the children know that these fun events are the reward for a job well done. A party or outing may be an award in an attendance drive, or for a good rehearsal or a good performance in a service.

Recruiting New Members

I have found that the awarding of a trophy helps a great deal in recruiting new members. He presents a "Choir Member of the Year" trophy at the end of each choir year.

In Junior and Primary choirs two women keep attendance records. The contest runs all year (the choir year should correspond with the Sunday school year). At the end of the year, the choir member with the best attendance record, and who has also brought the greatest number of visitors or new members, gets the trophy. Points may be taken away for bad conduct. The trophy should be engraved "Choir Member of the Year," stating the year and the names of the choir, the church, and the pastor. Many choir members work hard to bring new members and to always be on time for rehearsals in order to win this trophy. The trophy is not small or insignificant; it is a nice, big beautiful loving cup. It is usually presented to the winner in a Wednesday evening service.

The large Junior Choir of Northwest Baptist Church, Miami, Florida.

Discipline

While extra sponsors help a great deal with the discipline in children's choirs, the choir director should maintain order in the choir. Juniors, especially, can get out of hand very rapidly. Let them know who is boss, but, again and again, let them know that they are loved.

In the children's rehearsals, especially in Beginner and Primary choirs, there should be periods of relaxation. The children should be able to get a drink or use the restroom, but should be closely supervised.

Training

Start with Primaries and Juniors to instill a sense of faithfulness to choir practice and to performance in the church services. These groups can understand also a great deal about music fundamentals. Many have already learned them in music classes at school. Using a chalkboard, draw the different notes, rests, sharps, flats, staffs, etc., and use them for drill in these basics. If children learn some of these facts as Primaries, they will make much better Junior choir members. If they learn more as Juniors, they will make good Teenage choir members. And if they continue their training and accomplish more as Teenage choir members, they will make excellent Adult choir members. This is a strong point in favor of a graded choir program. The result, of course, is better choir members in every phase of the choir work.

Special Junior Ensembles

Often a junior choir will be blessed with several children of exceptional talent. Small ensembles can be formed with these children, adding to the variety and effectiveness of the total music program.

A junior girls' trio, for example, in a Wednesday evening service, can add a brightness rarely achieved. From a musical standpoint their singing may not be overwhelming, but because their parents are in the congregation, and because they exhibit talent and musical confidence, their contribution will be enjoyed.

This specialized training and experience at an early age will be invaluable, in years to come, in forming teen or adult ensembles.

Choir Mothers

Mothers of many of the children in the choirs will be glad to help in the rehearsal time and in any other way they are needed. Use them as choir mothers and choir sponsors.

Following is a summary of the thoughts of R. O. Stone, music director of the First Baptist Church, Jacksonville, Florida, concerning children's choirs:

CHILDREN'S CHOIRS

by R. O. Stone

The choirs of tomorrow will be no better than your training of today—the secret is "challenge." Our four-year-olds are challenged to learn at an early age that the Lord Jesus wants their little voices to glorify his name. Let's start even now to acquaint these little folks with musical knowledge. The six-, seven-, and eight-year-olds begin ear training through tone matching and learning the fundamentals of music. Here we introduce two parts in the form of countermelodies.

Junior boys and girls are a refreshing age to teach to sing for Jesus. Implant in their minds the real purpose of easy tone production, and they will naturally give you the fortissimo. Work on tonal placement, and these voices will be a thrill. Challenge this age with two- and three-part keyboard, along with conducting patterns, and you will stir excitement.

The cambiata age is a challenge! The junior high choir is the choir of changing voices. We should not push this age, but should present songs in an easy SAB range for a challenge to these wonderful teens.

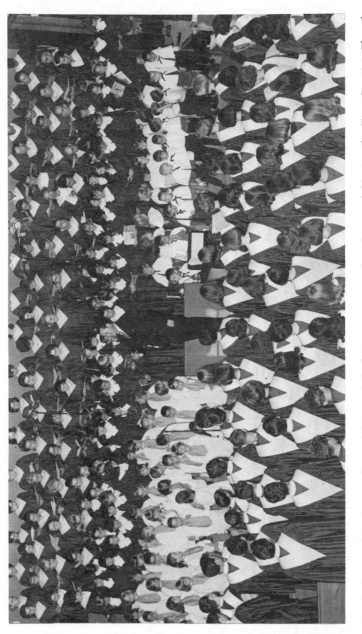

R. O. Stone with the members of his graded choir program gathered around him at the First Baptist Church of Jacksonville, Florida.

In a church with a planned program of graded activities for children through teens, lives are being built around the gospel through music. A feeder of ready-trained musicians for youth and adult choirs is being trained, to be a joy to the church and the heavenly Father as they sing for souls.

A music survey is a valuable means of promoting and enlisting for children's choirs. Focusing attention through the Sunday school and worship services, along with a mail-out of your designated age, time, place, and leadership, will encourage parents and children to be a part of the choral program.

Use exciting methods to which children respond, such as "Carnival for Choristers," "Circus for Songsters," and "Choir Round-Up," to aid in getting the children to the church for the beginning of your children's choirs.

God has blessed us in a wonderful way, giving us an enrollment of 1,043 in our music ministry at the old downtown First Baptist Church of Jacksonville, Florida.

10

Special Choirs and

Small Ensembles

SEVERAL different kinds of special choirs and small ensembles can be used to add variety and interest to a service.

The Men's Chorus

A men's chorus can be used very effectively on Father's Day or for a big patriotic program or service. The singing of men is especially enjoyed by most everyone. Many feel there is nothing more beautiful or more soul-stirring than a forceful song by a men's chorus in four-part harmony. It rouses an audience. Most choirs have a built-in men's chorus. Actually, the men's section of the adult choir can be used as a male chorus. Or they can be combines with some older teenagers from the teen choir. Preparing such a group to sing takes time and extra effort on the part of the men and the director, but the result is worth the effort.

Usually, eight, twelve, or sixteen voices, with two, three, or four voices on each part, make up this music group. Often a radio choir is composed of twelve to sixteen voices. The famous Sixteen Singing Men are extensively used because of their great ability, and because of the magnificent performances obtained when sixteen talented, well-trained men have spent time in rehearsals.

The Ladies' Choir

A ladies' chorus is especially appropriate to use on Mother's Day or other similar occasions. Ladies singing in three- and four-part harmony seem to have a very pleasing effect on any audience.

This can be a huge trio with several ladies singing first soprano, several more the second-soprano part, and another group, alto. Ordinarily three-part harmony is used with this group, but occasionally four- and five-part harmony can be very effective.

Combined Choirs

In 1966 on the Christmas program of the First Baptist Church of Hammond, one number was sung by the combined Adult, Teenage, Junior, and Primary Choirs. Approximately 250 people lifted their voices together in a thrilling Christmas song, a special arrangement of "Joy to the World." It had a spine-tingling effect on the audience.

Another such occasion in that church was the opening of the 1968 Pastors' School, for which I directed a combined choir of 225 voices in the Hammond Civic Center. This choir was especially formed for that meeting from the Adult and Teen Choirs, augmented by other adults enlisted for the occasion.

Another type of large special choir is one combining choirs from several churches, to be used in a cooperative evangelistic effort, such as a city- or county-wide revival meeting. A great deal of organizing and planning goes into forming such a choir, but the results are rewarding and make an indelible impression on those who see and hear it.

Senior Citizens' Choirs

In a church where there are a large number of senior citizens, a "Golden Age" choir could be formed. They would bless the

Three hundred voice combined choir of a union evangelistic campaign in the Atlanta Civic Center. Lindsay Terry is directing the choir.

Large combined choir, directed by Lindsay Terry, singing for the opening of the 1969 Pastor's School in Hammond Civic Center, Hammond, Indiana.

hearts of the hearers, and would themselves receive a great deal of companionship from such an effort, as well as a feeling of accomplishment.

A Deaf Choir

More and more churches are ministering to the vast number of deaf persons in their communities. The deaf love to "sing" and can do so, quite beautifully, in the sign language. A deaf choir must, of course, sing along with other hearing singers, but the uniqueness of such an arrangement adds greatly to an exciting music program.

Small Ensembles

Besides adding brightness and variety to the church service not obtained in any other way, small ensembles allow large numbers of people to participate in the special music. The singers for triple trios, sextets, duets, quartets, trios, ladies' choruses, mixed quartets, and special smaller choirs should be carefully chosen, and should have regular weekly rehearsal periods.

When several ensembles are used alternately, the musical selections can be well rehearsed for a professional performance that will add dignity and sincerity to the services. In a church where this is true, a visitor may attend for a month and never hear the same group or soloist perform twice. It is impressive to visitors, and a great attraction to the church.

Kinds of Groups

1. *Trios.* Trios are usually made up of three female voices, although this is not imperative. The three female voices would be soprano, second soprano, and alto. A mixed trio could be soprano, alto, and tenor, or an alto, tenor, and baritone group could be most popular when well blended.

2. *Quartets.* These can be either men's, ladies', or mixed quartets. The most thrilling group to most church audiences is the male

quartet, with a vibrancy and strength not found in ladies' or mixed quartets.

3. *Sextets.*   Some weaker or less-trained voices can be used in the ladies' group (soprano, second soprano and alto). Any treble arrangements can be used but a ladies' trio does best with trio arrangements.

The ladies' sextet has proven popular, possibly because it features six ladies, each of whom has friends in the congregation; but also, because of the group's size, the rendition has a large, full sound.

Blend is relatively no problem in a ladies' sextet, though it might always be improved, if the right techniques are used. In any group each singer should listen to those standing next to her and, without going too far afield of right techniques, try to blend or imitate the tone of that person. Constant awareness of the need for a better blend will cause the group to "feel" together and blend more readily. As a general rule, any ensemble must sing together for a period of time before they begin to "feel" together and thus greatly improve their performances.

The standing arrangement of this (or any) ensemble is important. The physical appearance of the group should not take away from the message of the song. Still maintaining blend and balance, the taller persons should be placed on the outside and the shorter persons at the center, or vice versa.

4. *The Triple Trio.*   This is, as the title suggests, a group of nine voices with three on each part. As with a sextet, other arrangements can be used, but this group is very effective when using regular trio arrangements. Three people singing each part achieve a confidence and security because each supports the other. Less-trained voices can participate if at least one good, strong, well-trained voice is the leader in each section of the triple trio.

The standing arrangement of a group this large needs careful planning. The approach to the platform should be worked out and rehearsed prior to the service time. For variety, use several different standing arrangements, other than just a semicircle.

As a teen ensemble, six girls and three fellows may form a triple trio; with the young men singing the melody, three of the young ladies singing second soprano, and the remaining three singing alto. Many fine three-part choir arrangements (SAB) can be used by this group. Regular three-part treble arrangements can also be used.

5. *The Octet*.   While this ensemble can be a double men's quartet, it is usually a double mixed quartet. Range and degree of quality depend on the talents of the individual singers. A carefully picked group may be able to do difficult arrangements not used by the choir with less training.

6. *Miscellaneous Groups*.   There are other groups that can be used effectively to provide variety in a music program, such as a senior citizen's choir, an elderly (over 65) ladies' chorus, and a Spanish choir.

Choosing the Voices

Choose ensemble singers very, very carefully, well in advance of the actual enlisting. A good choir director should be able to know individual voices before making selections for a particular group. It is difficult to remove a person chosen for a group, if he or she does not work into the group adequately. Therefore, great care in selection should be used.

In a regular choir rehearsal, ensemble possibilities may be asked to sing a special portion of the arrangement. The director can obtain some idea of the quality and blendability of their voices. These singers may be chosen at random to sing these parts. In this way, a quartet or trio may be put together without the participants being aware that they are auditioning for a part in a special ensemble.

The Rehearsal Times

Each group should have its own rehearsal time every week. If available, a captain or leader assigned to the group should meet with them, as well as an accompanist. They should be told well in advance of their next performance, so they can have their song so well rehearsed that their preparation will be evident.

Many times it is effective to designate one evening a week as music night at the church. The choir will rehearse; before or after choir practice, several groups may also have their rehearsals. This keeps people from having to spend too many nights away from their families. Also, some rehearsals may be scheduled before or after regular services; after the Wednesday evening service is a good time to practice.

Strict adherence to rehearsal times is of the utmost importance. It requires a great discipline on the part of director and members, but it will pay off in a quality music program that will bless the members of the church and add to the variety and effectiveness of the services.

At each practice rehearse at least three or four numbers. The major part of the rehearsal could be spent on the number to be performed next, and lesser amounts of time on other numbers for future performances. One or two numbers should be kept in readiness at all times so that a given group might be called on in an emergency if deemed necessary by the director. Numbers performed well in the services should be reviewed often, and repeated occasionally. It is a pity for a group to spend hours in rehearsal, perform a number that is evidently a blessing and help to the congregation, and then put it on a shelf and never use it again.

Performances

Because these special groups perform on the platform before the whole congregation each individual should be approved by the pastor (see Chapter 3).

Each group should approach the platform in a professional manner, not slovenly or slipshod, but with eager anticipation of an opportunity to do a good job for Christ and be a blessing to the people. It should anticipate presenting a salvation message to the lost, or a Christian testimony to all. Good posture should be maintained at all times. Emphasis should be placed on this during rehearsal.

Wearing apparel should be modest and in good taste; many directors choose to have ensembles dress uniformly. This is very effective and gives the audiences an impression of the group's care and pride in its presentation (the writer has several dress-alike ensembles).

The microphone placement should be rehearsed well in advance so that each singer knows exactly which mike he is to face. The control engineer for the PA system should be briefed, also.

Never should the performances be showy or the performers display an attitude of cockiness. They should have a delightful pleasantness that says, "We are here to do a job and to do it correctly for the Savior."

Material

A great variety of music can be obtained for special ensemble. Some groups are at home with music with a definite rhythmic pattern, while others like materials with expression and a variety of interpretation. All materials should contain a Christian, biblical message.

All music should be approved by the music director—if for no other reason, to keep two groups from working on the same number at the same time. It would waste time for two groups to spend several hours in rehearsals, only to learn they had been working on the same numbers. It could happen.

Records

Records should be kept of each ensemble, the dates of their performances, the songs they have sung, and copies of the arrangements. This, of course, will require the time of a choir secretary and a good filing system.

11

Soloists

IN most evangelistic church services a part of the music program is the singing of at least one soloist. There are two main reasons for this: (1) people everywhere love to hear a single voice, and (2) it is much easier to have a soloist to sing than to combine voices in special ensembles. I am not advocating that a great number of soloists should be used, I am simply stating that a number *are* used in the average church.

A special solo number is usually performed just before the message. It is thought that perhaps a single voice can prepare the hearts of the people for the message more readily than a choir or an ensemble. Keeping in mind that a solo, tastefully rendered, can contribute greatly to an evangelistic service, there are some special aspects that should be considered.

The Testimony and Christian Experience of the Soloist

Any soloist who stands before a congregation to sing a message of Christ should have assurance that he has been born again. There should have been a time in his life when he realized that he was lost and yielded his heart and life to Jesus Christ. Many churches have paid soloists who are considered only for their beautiful voices and their musical renditions, with no mention made of their spiritual experience. They sing from the intellect and not from the heart. Again, the singer should be saved and mean sincerely the message he is singing.

The Musical Background of the Soloist

Many singers are born with a good "instrument" and can do an acceptable job as a soloist without formal training. For this wonderful gift any singer should be truly thankful. A soloist can better equip himself if he can find a good teacher and take some voice training. There are some basics that are essential to good singing.

It is good for a singer to be able to read music so that he can learn new material quickly, or so that he can thumb through a hymnal or songbook and pick out beautiful songs. It is also a definite advantage for a soloist to have the proper breathing technique. Ninety percent of good singing is proper breathing. More will be said in this chapter concerning breathing.

I have been a soloist for approximately eighteen years. It was not until my second year at college that I decided to study music seriously. After my first voice lesson, I asked my teacher, "Will I ever be able to sing a solo?" Her reply was, "If you are willing to work very long and very hard, you might one day be able to sing a solo, perhaps." I determined that I would work long and hard and accomplish this for Christ. The results were that I studied voice for approximately six years, five years under Donella Brown, at Tennessee Temple College. I practiced one song for three years before performing it in public—"The Lord's Prayer," by Mallott.

There is absolutely no short cut to becoming a good vocalist. It takes about five or six years for a young singer's abdominal muscles to position and harden so that he can rely on them to help him with breathing and breath control. The only reason that many singers cannot sing into their sixties and seventies is that they loose breath control. Any singer who slacks off and does not continue these exercises will diminish in his ability to sing well.

Any singer who has not had training should avail himself of a voice coach or teacher to help him with these basic exercises. Every Christian singer should strive to be his best. One need not be second-rate just because he believes the Bible.

The Choice of a Song

The soloist's choice of the right song is of utmost importance to the service. Several things should be considered in choosing a song:

1. *Type of Service.* In an evangelistic service where reaching the lost is the primary goal the soloist should choose a song with a testimony or salvation message. All too often, soloists choose songs that are particularly suited to their voices, but are lacking in the really scriptural message needed for the occasion.

Some singers have what they call "sugar stick," songs that they have done many times before. These should be used very prayerfully in soul-winning services.

Songs of a general nature should be used for other than soul-winning services. They should be chosen carefully, but more variety is allowed in other services.

2. *Variety.* All soloists should try to learn a variety of songs so that their repertoire might be enlarged, enabling them to sing the proper selections on many different occasions.

3. *New Songs.* All soloists should be constantly searching for new songs. Homer Britton suggested to me in the summer of 1953, "Learn at least one new song every day." This practice would add an amazing variety and depth to any singer's storehouse of material.

The Choice of a Soloist

The music director should consult with the pastor before choosing persons as soloists for church services. Just as the members of the different ensembles should be chosen in consultation with the pastor, the soloists should have his approval. Often, because of personal counseling, the pastor will have certain information concerning an individual that is not known to the music director. This information could allow him to better choose and select persons who should appear on the church platform.

HELPFUL HINTS FOR A VOCALIST

by R. O. Stone

1. *Enunciation.* Diction should always be natural. Avoid pronouncing words in an affected manner. Sing the words as you would speak them. Singing is, after all, only sustained speech. A simple rule to follow is to put the ed's, t's, s's, etc., on the ends of the words. Always be CONSCIOUS of this. Another good rule is to overemphasize the pronunciation of your words. This will not be noticed by the audience, but they will be able to understand the words.

2. *Rhythm.* You will find that you are less apt to depend on others if you develop a strong rhythmic response to music. There is no better way to solve this problem than to simply count 1, 2, 3, 4, or whatever the time signature. For example: In 4/4 time, a whole note gets 4 beats; a half note gets 2 beats; a quarter note gets 1 beat; a dot following a note gets half again the value of the note itself; and an eighth note gets ½ beat.

You can apply this to other time signatures. Practice by tapping your foot and reading the song aloud, in correct rhythm, all the way through. (When in choir, try to follow the tempo set by the conductor.)

3. *Correct Breathing Habits.* Establishing correct breathing habits is a most important function if you are to receive the greatest benefit from your voice.

High-chest breathing does not fill the lungs to capacity. Excess tension in the upper-chest muscles affects the muscles around the larynx and inhibits the proper action of the vocal cords.

Think of yourself as a chimney on top of a house. Think of

this "chimney" as beginning in the abdomen, going up through the throat and out the mouth. Smoke does not come from the part of the chimney you see on the outside of the house, but rather from down deep in the fireplace inside the house. The same process can be applied to breathing. Breathe from down deep, where there is an abundant supply.

Poor breathing habits hinder tone production, tone quality, and the blending of voices. In singing, it is necessary to use the muscles around the entire midsection of the body, as well as the diaphragm. An excellent device is to bend over (from a standing position) until the upper part of the body is parallel with the floor. By placing the hands on the waist, the "feel" of correct breathing can be realized from this position. Try it!

After you have a conception of proper breathing, you must become "breath-conscious." Then *practice, practice, practice!*

4. *Attacks and Releases.* Learning the precision of attacks and releases is a most essential requirement in the training of a voice for effective solo work. These attacks and releases depend upon the attentiveness of the person and his response to the rhythmic pulsation of the music.

5. *Good Posture.* Posture is most important. You should sit or stand erect at all times. The head should be relaxed, with the chin in.

Strive to maintain good posture, adequate breath support, a loose, flexible jaw, and a tone with a high, forward resonance.

Never sing as loudly as possible. Do not push, but let the tones flow as easily as possible, always listening to the accompaniment.

Anticipate extremely high notes, low notes, and the ends of phrases.

12

Accompanists

IN any music program the most important position other than the music director is held by the accompanist. The magnitude of this position cannot be stressed too much in terms of helpfulness to the total music program. A music program may actually rise or fall with the accompaniment. Just as a car with a governor installed cannot be driven more than an established speed, the music program cannot rise higher than the accompaniment will allow.

Most churches cannot control, to a great extent, the ability of those who play the instruments because, for the most part, these are volunteers, and the number of accomplished instrumentalists is always extremely limited. Fortunate is the church with an abundance of well-trained musicians to play the piano or organ. Yet there are certain qualifications that should be imposed on any church accompanists. These qualifications should be initiated by the pastor and implemented or enforced by the music director.

Spiritual Qualifications

Since being a church accompanist is a real spiritual ministry, certain standards or measurements should be adhered to by those who play the instruments.

1. *Conversion Experience.* Countless churches, lacking accompanists from their congregation, hire an outsider to come in to play the instruments. This individual may not be questioned as to his conversion experience or even whether or not he is a Christian. This person is at a definite disadvantage in the service. Because he does not understand spiritual things, such as the moving of the Holy Spirit, he is not able to fit in with the mood of a service or adapt himself to the wishes of the pastor in behalf of the spiritual well-being of the service. Every accompanist should be able to point to a time when he came to know Jesus Christ as his personal Savior.

2. *Dedication to the Task.* Fortunate indeed is the music director who has an accompanist who will share the responsibility for making the musical portion of the service all that it can and should be. This is called "dedication." Many music directors suffer because the accompanist feels drafted into a situation that is undesirable. It is impossible for this person to hide this attitude completely. When an accompanist accepts a position, it should be with the intent to do the best job possible for as long as the task is continued. Like the pastor or music director, the accompanist is on display; his attitudes and expressions are carefully scrutinized by the audience.

Accompanists should take their tasks seriously enough that they will daily pray for God's help in performing this important task.

3. *A Spirit of Cooperation.* Any pianist or organist must bear in mind that someone else—the music director or pastor—actually determines what shall be done, and when and where it shall be done. Willingness to cooperate and to make the total program run smoothly is a prerequisite to good accompaniment. This does not mean that the music director always makes the right decisions, but that the accompanist, having taken the job, has

enough confidence in him to follow his leadership and to be exemplary in his cooperation.

On the other hand, many accompanists are mistreated and taken advantage of because of (1) a lack of other accompanists; (2) their spirit of cooperation; (3) an ability that is perhaps superior to the other accompanists in the church.

As stated earlier, accompanists should be given music in advance, so they will not be embarrassed when asked to play it for rehearsals or for performances. Also they should be alerted in advance as to the schedule of services or planned events, so that their family schedules and plans will not conflict with the schedule of church activities.

Cooperation is a two-way street; each person in the music program—especially the accompanists and the music directors—should respect the schedules of the others. Just as the music director has certain responsibilities in scheduling, so does the accompanist. During vacation or at other times when it is necessary to be absent, the accompanist should alert the music director or the pastor in advance, so that the proper substitute might be secured. This allows for a minimum interruption of the flow of the church service. It is all-important that the services do not suffer.

4. *A Sense of Ministering.* Numbers of accompanists feel definitely called of God to play the piano or organ, and to them it is definitely a ministry, a vocation, part of a divine plan.

Musical Qualifications

How sad for an accompanist to feel keenly aware that he should be helpful to the Lord's work, only to realize that as a child he neglected his musical training. Of course, spiritual fervor and desire to help do not cause a person to play more expertly.

Musical Training

Musical training especially keyboard training, is important at an early age. This age differs, but many music teachers feel that children have by then reached a stage when they can discipline themselves to practice and can understand necessity for hours of practice. Parents or adult leaders may recognize native music ability, or lack of it, in the Junior age. Many parents, zealous for training their children in the finer things of life, start young children of five or six on piano lessons, only to have them become discouraged and quit after a year or so. They have not reached a maturity that allows them to understand the necessary practice; because they are driven to practice, they become repulsed. In many cases they are ruined from ever enjoying the piano or organ because of a psychological barrier built up in those tender, impressionable years.

Because neighbor children have begun to take lessons, many parents push their children into private instruction and sink tremendous amounts of hard-earned money into lessons that are a waste because of the immaturity of the children. There are exceptions to this, but they are just that, exceptions and not the rule. Some of the finest accompanists in the world began their ventures on the keyboard at the tender age of four or five, but they are rare exceptions.

Some concert artists did not begin their musical training with private instruction until age fifteen or sixteen, and some outstanding church accompanists even much later in life. Any person with an innate ability to play a keyboard instrument does not completely lose this ability with the passing of years. Were it cultivated earlier, a much better accompanist would be the result. One reason that youth or adults often make tremendous pianists is that they are old enough to realize the importance of musical training, and they are completely dedicated to the task.

College Training

Most college students who are music majors, had their music training years before and college is a more concentrated continuation of that training. However, in some cases music training is begun during college years. Such was the case with me. Except for a few trumpet lessons in grades five and six, my serious music training was not begun until after my freshman year in college. Most church accompanists may have little or no college training, but churches that can obtain the services of a college-trained musician are fortunate indeed. There are, however, many cases where those without college training are more technically qualified and give themselves to the task better than the college-trained person.

Personal Improvements in Musical Ability

Just as in every other vocation, those who succeed and who go beyond the ordinary are those who are constantly seeking ways and means of personal improvement in their ability and in their attitude toward the task at hand. Once an accompanist loses the desire to play a particular selection with more meaning, with more delight, and with more spiritual inspiration, then he should quickly and quietly find some other way to make himself useful in the cause of Christ. But the accompanist who is completely dedicated to the task and willing to give himself to the task, will find the way and will spend the required hours to do what he seeks to achieve. Following are some suggestions for improving the musical ability of an accompanist:

1. *Listening to and Observing Others.*   In order to play beautifully, an instrumentalist must know what really beautiful playing is. He must hear beautiful playing, not simply to imitate, but to be inspired and to be educated to recognize accomplished performances. Pianists should learn to evaluate and to analyze the performance of others. One excellent way for an accompanist to hear and evaluate others is by recordings. Every accompanist should have a record player and a collection of good instrumental albums. These give an idea of technique, and furnish inspiration so vital to accompanists.

2. *Reading.*   Accompanists should take advantage of the numerous volumes written concerning good accompaniment and the many select articles in periodicals. There are advantages to this type of reading for them: Attitudes and philosophy are often dis-

cussed; new concepts are presented; suggestions in scheduling rehearsals and private instructions are also discussed; young accompanists are often given encouragement through the writings.

3. *Reaching for Goals.* As in other professions, an accompanist who does all that he or she sets out to accomplish must set goals that are attainable, yet require work. Discipline must be exercised in this area. Goals might be set concerning length of practice time, number of new pieces, or the mastering of difficult compositions. All compositions may not be used in the music program. Learning "hard-to-play" selections increases ability to do a masterful job at complicated compositions.

Concerning practice, each accompanist should set a definite, possible amount of time for his daily rehearsals. Setting a goal that he cannot reach will cause discouragement and be more a problem to him than value. Nothing will take the place of a regular practice to sharpen the mind and the reflexes continually. No Christian in a Christian vocation should become satisfied with his accomplishment, but should always strive to improve his ability for Christ.

By learning new selections an accompanist can save himself a great deal of difficulty in the future and, in some cases, embarrassment. During the practice and as a part of the practice time an instrumentalist should play through two or three new selections or unfamiliar songs. He might repeat favorite new ones so that he might be familiar with them for the future. An accompanist can help the music director by calling his attention to unusual selections thus learned during practice. Many directors do not play the piano well and find it more difficult to learn new selections than a good pianist.

Learning to Select Music

An accompanist in tune with God, who has the good of the service at heart, will be of greater value and be able to make a more spiritual contribution to the services in selecting music. Music selection is of utmost importance. It should be done prayerfully, with the congregation always in mind. The ability to always select the most appropriate songs is an art, albeit a developed art, which cannot be taken lightly.

It is not enough for an accompanist to sit down and begin to play, flipping from one selection to another, either at a funeral or during preludes or postludes for an evangelistic service. An accompanist who has no more love for his place of service than to give it absolutely no forethought should carefully consider giving up his position. The wise pastor or music director who hires or enlists an accompanist will make sure that this subject is covered in the employment interview.

A wise accompanist will consider the musical background of the majority of the audience to which he will be playing. Some will be more classical-oriented, some will favor evangelistic music, and some will love and appreciate "country" music, which has increasing popularity. Every accompanist can familiarize himself with any of these areas so he can accomplish an end result, and, at the same time, have his music enjoyed by the audience. This is not to say that only classical selections should be played for the classical-oriented audience, or that those more familiar with the "country sound" should hear only that which they are accustomed to. But all accompanists can, with a little effort, include playing in all three areas, and do it with good taste and a fervent, warm heart.

In some specific areas (three already mentioned), an accompanist must exercise great care in selecting the music that he plays.

Preludes

As most audiences enter the auditorium for a service either the piano or the organ, and occasionally a church orchestra, will be playing. First impressions of the church are being formed by guests who have never been there before. If they were not met at the door by an usher, then the instrumentalist is helping them to form an opinion of the church. It is very important that these first impressions be favorable. The visitor may be actually deciding, "I think I shall enjoy this service, because the music is going to be great." While it is to be hoped the impressions are never otherwise, I am fearful that they are.

The hearts of the people need to be prepared for the service. This preparation will be continued in the song service and other activities prior to the message, but it is begun during the prelude. The audience needs to detect in the accompanist a sincerity that flows out through his music.

Preludes set the tone for the service; therefore, in an evangelistic service, prelude music should be evangelistic. Each Sunday morning service should direct a great deal of attention to winning souls to Christ, because more lost people are in the Sunday morning services. The accompanist should play familiar songs with a message of salvation or consecration easily recognizable to the hearers. He should choose songs with a variety of rhythmic or time signatures: i.e., he should not choose two or three songs in succession with four-four timing, or several in succession with three-four timing. All of the songs must not be slow, nor should all of the songs be lively. For instance, "Blessed Assurance" could be followed by "My Jesus, I Love Thee"; or "I Will Sing the Wondrous Story" could be followed by "Amazing Grace."

It is true that many disagree with the old philosophy behind this approach, but the churches of today, by and large, have become more interested in building an "atmosphere" than in winning the lost to Christ.

Baptismal Background Music

In many churches this would not be an important aspect of the organist's ministry, because baptismal services are few and far between. But in most of the aggressive Baptist churches there is a baptismal service almost each week, and, in many cases, in every service. In some churches in which there are 15 to 20 people baptized each Sunday or even more, the background music for the baptismal service takes on a great deal of importance. It should be played softly, so as not to detract in any way from the service. It is truly "background" music.

Songs of salvation and obedience should be selected. Any song that speaks of the death, burial, or resurrection of Christ would be appropriate for a baptismal service. Perhaps most appropriate is the gospel song "Trust and Obey," yet it is seldom used as background music for a baptismal service.

Donella Brown, chairman of the Music Department, Tennessee Temple School, Chattanooga, Tennessee, gives on the following pages her ideas concerning good accompaniment in church services.

ACCOMPANIMENT

by Donella Brown

The invitation time is the most important part of the service. The hymns and special music have been given to prepare the hearts of the people, and there has been the preaching of God's Word. Then comes the invitation. Many services have been spoiled and the Spirit of God has been unable to work effectively because the organist was not alert during this time.

Perhaps the preacher announces an invitation hymn, and the organist is not ready. Maybe she has gone to sit with her family in the congregation and has to walk to the organ, rustle through the hymnal to find the page and the key—and then give a long introduction! By this time the atmosphere has changed and the whole mood of the service has been broken, giving the devil a chance to detract the sinner's mind from the message.

Ask the pastor and song leader what is expected for an introduction for the invitational song. Generally, a solid chord for pitch is all that is needed. No time is lost and the spirit of the service is not broken. It is a help for the organist to have a list of the hymns most used, listing the keys and page numbers if the music is needed. Many organists mark these hymns in their book with paper clips so they are easy to find.

Invitation hymns should be played in a different manner from the militant hymns or choruses we use. This is a time of pleading with men's hearts to accept God's great gift of salvation through Christ Jesus his Son, and anything other than a spirit of prayerfulness and thoughtfulness is not honoring to our Lord, whom we serve.

An organist or pianist should work with the song leader concerning tempo. The song leader should lead, not the instrument. But the accompanist should not drag behind, but rather try to sense the mood and rhythm. If a spirit of cooperation is achieved, then the accompanist will be able to anticipate these things and can set the right tempo. A song leader should never have to make a drastic change in tempo when he begins to lead the congregation.

Above all, watch the leader. If he wants to vary the rhythm, the instrument should stay with him.

Be sure to check with the other instrumentalists as to keys. Some people do not like to play in keys with more than one sharp or two flats. Often when brass instruments are used, all songs written in sharps are played in flats for their convenience, since all B-flat instruments must transpose a whole step higher than written.

These things should all be settled before the service begins, so the organ will not play the introduction in three sharps, only to have the piano begin in four flats.

One note of caution: With congregational singing play the harmony that is written. Remember the people in the audience are singing and trying to follow what they see on the staff. If the accompanist decides to try out some new harmonies to the tune, it distracts and confuses them, to say nothing of the other instrumentalists.

In some churches it is customary to have an interlude before the last verse of each hymn. Here again, you need to find out about this before the service to save embarrassment for all. The same rule applies to the use of the "amen" after the final verse.

When you finish your introduction, you should be on the tonic chord or "home" key. This gives the singers a feeling of security. Never finish on a chord which leaves them "dangling" and looking for their pitch.

Often the first four measures plus the last four measures bring you to the tonic or "home" key smoothly. Other times, you may use the first two measures plus the last two measures.

If you are uncertain about your introductions, practice them as you would your offertories. After all, you make the first announcement of the hymn for the congregation. From this they should have the pitch, the rhythm, and the whole mood of the hymn, and be ready to sing the first word when you finish. This they can't do if the "trumpet blows an uncertain sound."

13

Instrumental Ensembles

AN important musical experience for any church is to have an instrumental ensemble as a regular part of its music program. The attention and interest it attracts, and the services it renders, are an asset in almost any situation. While there may be cases when ensembles or bands would be inappropriate, there is a vast need for them.

It is possible for churches, especially large churches, to have and maintain these instrumental groups because of the extensive music program in the public schools. Almost every child has access to some specialized music training on an instrument.

Just as Christian youth put valuable academic lessons into Christ's service, they should put their music training to work for him. Music becomes a part of their lives, and their total lives belong to Christ. Musicians, pastors, and educational directors should search for every possible means to increase the effectiveness of the church in serving the community for God.

The Church Orchestra

The church orchestra, if available, should be used for every service of the church, so the congregation does not think some services are more important than others. If this is not possible, the orchestra should be used in the Sunday services instead of week-night services. Special revival services, conferences, or a vacation Bible school parade or rally are other occasions for using a church band or orchestra.

Instrumentation

The church orchestra is made up of whatever instruments are available among church membership, because every person who plays an instrument should have opportunity to use it in Christian service. Often it requires special arranging to make the orchestration suitable for the variety of instruments, but this is not too difficult for experts such as band directors, orchestra leaders, and music faculty members. A balanced sound may be obtained with almost any combination of instruments, within the bounds of reason, and with time and effort.

Time and space will not be devoted here to technical instruction for building an orchestra or combining instruments, because whole volumes on this are available to any music director or orchestra conductor.

Personnel

The personnel of the church orchestra or band should meet the same requirements as choir members or ensemble personnel concerning their testimony and faithfulness to the church. After these considerations, their musical ability is of prime importance.

It may be advisable to have both a junior and senior instrumental group, because many grade school children now play instruments, yet their accomplishment is not sufficient for them to make a contribution to a church service. The music of these groups should be as professional as possible; therefore, a less experienced group might have an incentive to work hard to develop their ability, in order to be promoted to a more experienced group. No person with the ability and a desire to serve Christ should be denied the privilege and opportunity of doing so. Some improvising might have to be done, but usually a place can be made for everyone with ability and the willingness to serve.

Materials

Most major music publishers of band music have some sacred music, hymns and gospel songs, orchestrated and available. Also, many major Christian publishers are orchestrating hymnals and publishing scores for choir arrangements. The list of these publishers is as follows:

PUBLISHERS FOR ORCHESTRATIONS

Hope Publishing Company
Carol Stream
Illinois

Lillenas Publishing Company
Kansas City
Missouri

Zondervan Publishing House
Grand Rapids
Michigan

Word, Incorporated
Waco
Texas

Smaller Ensembles

Groups with fewer numbers are usually chosen from the larger orchestra, because they are more experienced, capable musicians who are willing to spend extra time and effort in a specialized ensemble. In many churches such specialized groups are often used to the exclusion of a church orchestra or large band. Some directors feel that smaller ensembles make a more professional, dignified contribution to the church service. Consider the following groups for use in the church.

Brass Ensembles

Made up of trumpets, trombones, and baritone horns, these groups are probably the most numerous and the most popular of the smaller groups; especially useful are trumpet duets or trios.

If the instruments are available, a brass quartet of two trumpets, a trombone, and a baritone is absolutely unsurpassed in adaptability and blend. A trumpet and trombone also make a good combination. In such a duet the trombone should take the higher harmony and the trumpet the melody or lower harmony.

Woodwinds

The closeness of the harmony of saxophones and clarinets and their blend cannot be improved upon, no matter which combination of instruments is used. Strings also blend well with clarinets and some saxophones. There is a wide range of instruments that can be experimented with in the woodwind and the string sections.

Brass and Woodwind Combinations

Often a church may only have one or two brass instruments and a few woodwinds; with a good deal of work and effort, these may be used together to great advantage, to thrill and inspire the congregation.

Preparation and Materials

No efficient or worthwhile instrumental group can be achieved without regular weekly scheduled rehearsals. The best time for an orchestra to practice is just prior to performance. If this is not possible, a warm-up period is mandatory just before the performance, just as for the choir or vocal ensembles. The orchestra and the smaller ensembles should enter into this service of Christ with a great desire to be faithful to the task.

A wealth of music is available for small groups such as the trumpet trio, brass quartet, or string ensembles. Many times a music director will have to obtain materials and adapt them to his particular situation. He should contact local music stores and ask to see their catalogs from the various publishers for instrumental music. Local band directors or other music directors can also make suggestions for locating materials. A talented music director can often arrange his own materials for smaller ensembles after studying a book on orchestration.

Special Instrumental Accompanying

Choir accompaniment is usually done with piano and organ, but the use of other instruments can be very exciting as they lend themselves to wonderful performances: trumpets, violins, vibraharps, and trombones. Often choirs are accompanied by church orchestras, but smaller groups of instruments are also used to augment or enhance a selection. For instance, a violin may carry an obligato part, or a trumpet trio may play a fanfare and short interludes. Violins may be used to give an effect of soothing or serenity. Each instrument may be used in introductions and during interludes and closings for special added appeal.

Other special effects may be produced by using such instruments as the vibraharp or marimba for "bells." The marimba and vibraharp may also be used with numbers that effect an atmosphere of prayer or serenity or the bliss of heaven. Possibilities are endless. Suffice it to say that all persons who play instruments well should have the opportunity to do so, even if such opportunity must be manufactured. The total result is a music program with good variety that will be a blessing and inspiration to all who hear.

Eddie Evans, music director of Northwest Baptist Church, Miami, Florida, has a fine church orchestra and shares these methods of developing such a group.

THE CHURCH ORCHESTRA

by Eddie Evans

The first thing to consider in forming an orchestra in a local church is the interest of the people. Would an orchestra add to or take away from the existing musical program? Would it enhance any part of the preaching services? Would it draw support from the pastor and the people? These matters should be evaluated in the planning stages of the orchestra.

For several weeks prior to the first scheduled meeting of the orchestra, promotion must be made through every means in your church: bulletins, the church paper, announcements from the pulpit, and at choir rehearsals, and any other media which might arise. Get the new ministry before the people. During this time be sure to have applications available in the church office, choir rehearsal room, music office, ushers' stations, and on your person.

Announce the first rehearsal and plan it big! This will make or break the future ministry of the orchestra. For the first few weeks rehearse only the congregational songs to be used on Sunday. This builds confidence in those who may have not played the instrument in fifteen years. Do not present a special number at the beginning of the orchestral ministry. It is good to whet the musical taste buds of the people for several weeks, during which time the orchestra is continuing to rehearse congregational songs and play them as accompaniment during the Sunday services. When both the orchestra members and the listening audience are ready for a special presentation use, as the first piece, a variation of an old, easily recognized hymn.

Once the orchestra is rehearsing regularly and performing periodically, its true effectiveness will be realized. Folk will be thrilled and excited with this new phase of church music. Naturally, every local situation is different, but at Northwest Baptist Church in Miami we have found the orchestra to be another arm of the ministry.

14

Music in the Services

A GREAT deal of work is carried on and a great number of hours are spent in rehearsal, all of which culminates in one place and at one time: the services of the church. A great deal of money, time, and effort goes into making the music program what it ought to be, in order that the presentation might lift the hearts of the people to the Lord and bless and inspire them; therefore, the services are all-important. Each week hundreds of people come to their churches and spend hundreds of hours in areas other than the music program. For instance, the bus workers spend countless hours knocking on doors, inviting people to come to the services. They get up on Sunday morning and get the buses started, go and make their rounds, bring hundreds of little children into Sunday school classes, and take them home again. All of this for one thing—the services. The janitor has carefully made sure the floors are scrubbed, the pews and the furnishings are dusted, the place is well lighted and ventilated, and everything is as it should be, for one thing—the services. The secretaries in the offices have typed many letters, done a great deal of mimeographing, answered the telephones many times, and met needs of all kinds, all pointing to one thing—the services. The pastor has spent hours preparing his sermon, so well that when he stands before the congregation they will give rapt attention; all of this for one thing—the services. Bonds have been sold to finance the erection of buildings, people have given sacrificially to help construct a place of worship, visitation has been carried on, hundreds of people have been invited to—the services.

I have said all of that to say this: the services are of utmost importance. Therefore the music program must make its greatest contribution in the services of the church. As the choir rehearses, the director must continually remind them that they are preparing for the important hours in the week—the services. The soloist, the special ensembles, and the accompanist must, in all their preparation, remember that it all culminates in the services. The kind of service that any church will be able to have depends largely on the music program. There are several things to consider in preparing the music for the service.

The Type of Service

A Soul-winning Service

This is a service in which the major emphasis is on reaching the lost for Christ. This may occur on Sunday morning, Sunday evening, Wednesday evening, or one night during a revival series. If the emphasis is on soul winning, the music should augment the service and should help to draw the minds of the people toward an evangelistic or soul-winning message. Songs about the cross, Jesus' power to save, or heaven and hell are songs to use in services of this nature. Not that a prayer song or one on some other subject may not be used, but the major emphasis of the music should be on evangelism for that particular service.

A Bible Study

These services could be in the church on Sunday evening or Wednesday evening, or even in a home: but the music should remind people of the Word of God and of the promises in the Word. If a particular Bible passage is chosen and announced beforehand, songs dealing particularly with that subject can be used most effectively. Preparation cannot be stressed too much at this point. If the song service is worth having, then it is worth putting time and effort into.

Practical Teaching Services

Often on Sunday evening pastors preach on subjects of a practical nature, such as the home, the relationship of the wife to the husband, the rearing of children, or personal soul winning. This gives opportunity to use some of the fine music on a particular topic; such songs are innumerable. These services also afford opportunity to have some songs that are unique in nature (such as Negro spirituals) or to have special youth presentations.

Little Things to Watch

Someone has wisely said, "If you are careful about the little things, the larger things will take care of themselves." While this may not be true in the strictest sense, it is a great philosophy to follow. As music director in several churches, I have learned to pay attention to minor details which seem insignificant, yet which, if unattended, may disrupt and distract in a service. A choir should watch carefully its posture and method of entering the choir loft, because these first impressions cause many visitors to determine if they are going to enjoy or just tolerate the service. Absolutely no glory can come to God through a sloppy choir performance, either from the standpoint of posture, attentiveness, or effort. I have often said in lecturing to music directors and music seminars, "We may not be able to have the best choir musically, but we can surely be the finest choir from the standpoint of effort in presentation."

The slightest turning of a head on the part of some choir member can distract a person in the audience from hearing part of the sermon.

Public Address Systems

Make sure that you have the finest public address system that you can afford, because an inexpensive public address system might let the audience hear, but distort the music and make it displeasing, ruining an otherwise fine performance. Therefore, it is mandatory that the choirs, ensembles, and soloists rehearse with the microphones, especially in a strange situation, so that proper balance and levels might be obtained for the service. Music directors should train their singers in using a microphone to best advantage, and in knowing how the public address technician controls the various aspects of the musical presentation. If this sounds too complicated and troublesome, a director would do well to seek another area of work. Every service should be to him the greatest single event, at that particular time, on the face of the earth. Until this is true his performances, and therefore the services, will lack something vital.

Appearance of Choirs

A measure of attention should be given to the way the choirs stand up and sit down and how they hold their books. They should stand and sit in unison. I prefer that all to the right of choir center (facing the choir) should hold the music in their right hand, using the left hand to turn pages or to steady the book. All to the left of center should hold the music in their left hand, using the right hand to turn pages and steady the book or folder.

The attitude and procedure of the smaller ensembles in approaching the platform and positioning themselves cannot be overstressed. This should be rehearsed so thoroughly they could rival an ROTC drill team. Nothing looks more sloppy or smacks of ill-preparedness more than the haphazard approach so many use in coming to the platform to sing. The pulpit should be approached with respect, dignity, and an assurance that shows complete readiness to sing. The singers should approach in a relaxed manner, but so confidently that it is evident even to small children that the group is well prepared to sing.

Personal appearance on the part of the men should be kept on a high plane. Unless robes are used, dress shirts, coats, and ties are proper for the men to wear and when robes are used, shirts and ties should be worn under them. Ladies should dress carefully, not attracting attention to themselves by flashy earrings, or gaudy apparel, if dresses are not covered by robes.

Communication with Ensemble Members

Make sure that all participants in the special groups are alerted in advance so that they may be prepared. Make sure that soloists and special singers (such as duet combinations and instrumental musicians) be notified or asked to sing or to present a number far enough in advance to give them ample time for preparation. Music activities planned far in advance result in a much better music program. When schedules become crowded because of last-minute notices or requests, it is human nature for some to take short cuts or to repeat something done previously, which otherwise would not have been used. Musicians lose confidence in a choir director who consistently fails to plan or to give proper notice of musical presentations.

Materials in Place

It is the job of the music director to make sure that the hymnals are distributed properly, in the pews and in the choir loft and on the speaker's platform. He need not do this personally, but he should make sure that it is done. Distribution should be made neatly and in proper order—another "little thing" that makes a good first impression on visitors.

The platform can easily become cluttered with loose pieces of music stuffed under the podium, tossed on the music director's chair or in the organ and piano pits, and even thrown on the instruments. Such disorder reflects lack of care for the material or for God's house; therefore, it should be avoided.

If choir music is not distributed in a rehearsal room before the service, the materials to be used should be made readily available to choir members, so the least effort is necessary for them to obtain their music and to move into position. Care should be taken after the service to collect the music and put it into the proper file. Again, this is not necessarily the job of the music director, but he should see that persons are appointed or elected to care for these matters.

Make sure the instruments are dusted, opened, and properly tuned for each service.

Numerous other things could be mentioned, but suffice it to say that a music director should adopt a philosophy of making sure that everything is "just right."

Avoiding Last-Minute Changes

Sometimes a program can be improved by changing some aspects of it at the last minute, but, as a general rule, this should be avoided. It is more often best to go with what is planned and worked on, than to change at a late moment at the whim or suggestion of a bystander. The risk of unnecessary repetition or ill-prepared music is present when such changes are allowed.

Changes may be altogether necessary at times, but God will then somehow make these things to work for his glory when we honestly strive to do the best job possible for him.

Coordinating the Total Music Program

Music in the services should have balance that will assure just the right amount of choir singing, the right special ensemble, and the right soloist. Nothing is more refreshing than such balance in the musical program. Many in the congregation have favorite groups, soloists, or choirs, but the music director should see to

Duet with large teenage choir as "back-up" group.

it that certain individuals are not overused, so people do not grow weary hearing them sing. *Variety* is the key word.

A good rule to adopt is to plan the music program a month ahead, making sure that groups and soloists perform in turn. Of course, some soloists and ensembles are superior and should be used more often, but not to the point that such frequent use is noticeable to all.

Harmony among the choir members and the special musicians should be sought, if it is not a reality, and should be guarded carefully. Here are some other aspects to consider in coordinating the total music program.

Congregational Singing

While congregational singing is discussed in another chapter, let it be noted here that this aspect of the music program should be carefully considered in setting up the total music department or outlining a single service. A weak link in the music chain often occurs at this point, and time should be spent making sure that this area of the service is unique and soul-stirring.

Leading Toward the Message

Often the speaker's topic is not discussed prior to his sermon, but when and if it is known far enough in advance, the music should enhance the message by emphasizing the subject about which the speaker is going to preach. The minds of the people must be captured from the outside world and brought into the service and pointed toward the message from the Word of God. Some singers are adept at setting up the congregation so the pastor can step in and continue, while others must work hard to acquire the ability.

It is seldom a good idea to have a choir number just before the message; it is more appropriate to have a small ensemble, a duet, or a soloist sing at that time. It should be moderate, not too slow or draggy, yet with not too much razz-a-ma-tazz or drama, keeping in mind that the Word of God is about to be presented.

The Order of Service

In some churches the order of service is so traditional that the service seems to proceed much more smoothly if it is followed. Some directors feel that this restricts the opportunity of the pastor to change with the mood of the service, while others do not. It is not my task to discourage or encourage the use of a printed order of service, but I prefer what I call "cue cards." These are 3 × 5 cards prepared before the service and distributed to the pastor, music director, pianist, organist, public address engineer, deaf interpreter, and head usher. Sample cue cards are pictured on the following page.

This is within the framework of "let all things be done decently and in order," yet it gives some latitude to the pastor and director without the audience feeling that they are departing from a set ritual. Every item on the card was placed there for a purpose and should be followed, but when the order needs to be varied, it can be done smoothly.

Cue cards prevent "dead spots" in the service. Nothing looks more amateurish than periods of time when the audience is watching and waiting for whatever is next. The cue card enables the soloist to be prepared to arise at the proper instant to take his place, assured that all leaders know exactly the time he is to perform. There is always a certain amount of pressure, even though a musician has sung for services for several years, and the cue card gives him opportunity to collect his thoughts prior to his participation in the services.

The music director usually makes out the cue cards and places them in the right positions. I place one on the piano and organ music stands, another on the table beside the pastor's seat on the platform, another in a hymnal on the pulpit stand, and three others with the public address engineer, the head usher, and the deaf interpreter. A supply of cue cards may be mimeographed

Sunday A.M. _____	Sunday P.M. _____	WEDNESDAY P.M. _____
Opening _____	Opening _____	CHOIR OPENING _____
Cong Song # _____	Cong. Song # _____	CONG SONG# _____
Prayer	Prayer	PRAYER
Choir	Choir	CONG SONG OR
Announcements	Announcements	SPECIAL NUMBER _____
Visitors _____	Visitors _____	
		WELCOME VISITORS
		ANNOUNCEMENTS
Cong Song # _____	Cong Song # _____	LETTERS: _____
Offering	Offering _____	_____
Scripture		_____
Cong Song # _____	Cong Song # _____	CONG SONG# _____
		OFFERING
		CONG SONG# _____
Special _____	Special _____	
Message	Message	MESSAGE _____
Invitation	Invitation	INVITATION
Cong Song # _____	Cong Song # _____	CONG SONG# _____
Baptism	Baptism	BAPTISM
Closing _____	Closing _____	PRAYER

with all divisions included, leaving space for weekly write-in information that changes with each service (see illustration).

Adapting to a Mood

Often a particular mood is deliberately created in a service; but, on the other hand, one may find himself in the midst of a service in which a mood has been created that was not at all planned, but is desirable as opposed to an atmosphere undesirable in a church service. These desirable moods or atmospheres are brought on by the Holy Spirit's moving in the midst of people, to bless their hearts and to bring lost ones to Christ. A music director in tune with God and those around him can recognize these moods and adapt to them, though the pastor must approve any changes in the order of service. The music director and musicians must accept the pastor's leadership, and, if changes are made, they must continue as though the total service had been planned that way. The music director and pastor should avoid announcing changes in the order of service or in the same facets of the program, lest audience attention be drawn from the mood of the service. These changes can often be made with a very slight gesture or movement on the platform if the pastor and music director work closely and in harmony. The possibility of changes makes it important for the instrumentalists always to be watching.

Too often, music directors become independent, forgetting that the pastor is the spiritual leader with a special gift from God to do his job and the supreme authority, humanly speaking, in the services. Musicians should be willing to change their plans or even to be deleted from the program on a moment's notice, if the pastor so desires.

The Check List

Whatever a person's duties, a checklist of responsibilities is of utmost importance. No individual can operate as efficiently without one as with one. Especially is this true for those working with many people and responsible for many details. Most people with normal intelligence can remember what they planned for, but some things may slip by. Use a checklist. Example:

1. Are the choir robes in place (if choir robes are to be used)?
2. Are the music folders in position?
3. Has all music for the service been placed in the folders and into the right hands?
4. Have the microphones been put in position and checked out as to the correct volume?
5. Have the cue cards been placed in the right positions?
6. Have I checked with the accompanist as to the offertory?
7. Are announcements noted and ready to be made?

This list could go on to cover all the items to be cared for. The items are then checked off one by one when you are sure they have been cared for. This is one difference between success and mediocrity.

15

Music for Television and Radio

FOR years—especially on Sunday morning—many radio stations have carried religious broadcasts. Music has played a great part in these broadcasts: in fact some programs consist wholly or largely of sacred music. Music presented on television or radio must be approached with a different attitude than for regular services, where the sense of hearing is not as critical because activities on the platform distract from what is heard. A portion of the listener's attention is absorbed by what he sees. But on radio, only the sense of hearing comes into play, and every chord and every word becomes critical; therefore, both the enunciation and the pronunciation must be precise if the audience is to get the desired message. One of the most difficult things for any choir to do, either on radio or in a live performance, is to sing together clearly, so they are heard and understood— though every choir director works toward this. Probably the master of choir pronunciation and enunciation is Fred Waring of "The Pennsylvanians" fame.

A chorus on television has the advantage of the sense of sight coming into play; in closeup shots, the lip movement helps viewers to understand the words. Much of our hearing is helped by lip reading.

There are several things to consider in preparing a music program for television or for radio.

Introductions and Closings

The most important part of any television or radio program is the introduction, which must capture the attention of the viewer or hearer immediately at the outset of the program. Although many television and radio programs are begun with speaking, most begin with a musical introduction. The safest thing to do for introductions and closings is to prerecord them and use one each week, changing it periodically as desired. This allows a more elaborate opening and closing than might ordinarily be possible. For instance, the television and radio broadcasts called "The Challenge of the Bible," which I produced employed an orchestra conductor and several members of the Atlanta Symphony Orchestra to record an orchestrated accompaniment to a vocal introduction and closing. This gives a bright, cheery sound as the programs open, competing somewhat with the best on any broadcast, whether on radio or television. The introduction and the closing should always be in keeping with the theme of the program. Some notable examples of this are "Back to the Bible," with an especially written theme by Eugene Clark; "The Challenge of the Bible," using the theme "Here Ye the Challenge" by John W. Peterson.

Vocal

Vocal introductions should be kept quite brief and should conform to the atmosphere and mood of the broadcast. Vocal introductions are especially effective if, after a short passage is sung, an announcer comes in over the portion being hummed, gives a very pointed, straightforward introduction to the program, and then lets the vocal close. There are endless combinations and selections to use for this purpose.

Instrumental

Instrumental introductions attract attention to the radio and television programs, but should be kept relatively short. If piano and organ are used, a tremendous amount of rehearsal should go into this particular performance. Orchestrations must be topnotch.

The Radio Choir

A radio choir can be more relaxed because they are not seen by the audience. Several things pertinent to this group must be watched carefully:

Voice Blend

Since the sense of hearing is brought predominantly into play, for proper effect the blend must be as impeccable as possible. This requires much rehearsal, and the music must be carefully selected. In order to give depth of sound, even with a small choir, the bass section should be larger than either of the other three. As on the piano or the organ, the bass section in the choir is the foundation for the group. It is virtually impossible to obtain the desired tones without full, broad lower parts.

Each person should listen intently to the singing of the person next to him and strive to blend his voice with that person. A really pleasing blend can only be obtained when a group has worked together over a long period, unless the group is chosen from top musically trained personnel.

If the hearers do not understand and get the message of the

words, then the organ and the piano might just as well play, omitting the singing.

Faithfulness

Nothing discourages a music director more than to have some people consistently absent from rehearsals and performances, especially for radio broadcasts. Each choir director should impress on those participating in a radio choir that this place of service extends outside of the church into the homes of shut-ins, elderly people, places of business, barber shops, and homes of the un-churched. It should be impressed on them that this is a rare privilege and an unparalleled opportunity which demands the faithfulness of every person in the group. When one individual is absent, he denies himself the opportunity of service, and his absenteeism is a detriment to the balance of the group. It is high time that those in Christian service realized that there is "only one life, 'Twill soon be past; Only what's done for Christ will last." Only heaven will reveal the tremendous good accomplished through faithfulness to the radio or television choir.

Choice of Music

Since most people who hear radio broadcasts or view the tele-casts are unsaved, it is a good idea to keep the music conserva-tive. It should be vibrant with life and, in some cases, lilting, but it must not remind them of the music of the world, causing them to wonder if there is a difference.

As in all services, the music should be evangelistic, with a message of salvation or a Bible-based exhortation.

Considerable thought should be given to the kind of audience aimed at. For instance, a program for the elderly should include a lot of old faithful hymns; older people enjoy hearing songs they knew in childhood. These bring back pleasant memories and re-fresh aging minds and hearts. Old age is a time of remembering; therefore, the songs of the past are most appropriate, although newer favorites can be used occasionally.

For a youthful audience, the lilting or rhythmic numbers should be used, for many of them would not even recognize the older hymns. Teens and young people look to the future, watching new advancements and trying to keep pace with modern times; hence the newer, brighter, more cheerful songs, done in a unique way, would appeal to them more. This is not an endorsement of gospel rock but a strong recommendation that the music be kept a little on the lighter side. Without using gospel rock, I have built some of the largest teen choirs in the nation.

Television Choir

Many suggestions for the radio choir are applicable also to television choruses. In addition, consider the following:

Posture and Physical Arrangement

Television audiences are quite critical; therefore, every movement of the television choir must be planned in the minutest detail. One person who is careless with hand or eye movement can distract somcone in the television audience. While the singers should be relaxed, even this attitude should be planned and rehearsed.

Viewers may not notice the size or position of a nicely arranged choir, but they will notice for sure whether or not the standing arrangement is careless. Placement of a very tall person next to a very short person can call attention to both. An extra two or three minutes at each taping or broadcasting session will ensure a pleasant-looking standing arrangement.

The position of the singers should be changed from time to time, to add to the total variety of the program.

Variety

As in the church service, radio and television programs should present a variety of singers and musical numbers. For a fifteen-minute program, the need is not as crucial as for a thirty-minute or hour broadcast, where the same group or the same soloist is used repeatedly. Change is essential, since one person will enjoy and receive a blessing from a number another person may not go for at all. With varied numbers, all come nearer finding something in the program that will speak to them and that they can relate to.

Technical Equipment

Pastors with a limited budget often begin radio ministries by using cheap, inferior recording equipment. While I am not promoting use of expensive equipment, purchased at tremendous sacrifices of the church, some counsel should be sought as to available equipment that will be adequate without costing an exorbitant amount. A young pastor or music director in charge of a radio ministry should check with the personnel at the broadcasting station concerning equipment, after time has been purchased. God's servants may only expect his blessings when they have done their best to present his Word in the finest way possible.

After suitable equipment has been selected, a good recording location should be found. If the radio studios themselves are not used, most church auditoriums provide a very good sound studio, and provide better instruments also.

Presentation of the Music

A most difficult aspect of music presentation for television is the proper facial expression of inexperienced amateur musicians. A good presentation can be accomplished if constant attention is paid such expression and projection. Many inexperienced singers feel self-conscious when they try to project themselves into the camera and to develop facial expressions that are cheerful and that present a message of happy Christianity. Once these inexperienced singers become accustomed to projection through facial expressions, it becomes easier. The best way to show them the need for improvement is to let them view the tapes immediately after recording. Another way is to urge them to be aware of facial expressions and projection when viewing other television programs, whether religious or secular. A major reason that amateur programs "turn off" so many viewers is that often a person endowed with a beautiful voice cannot communicate because of a lack of projection through facial expression.

Each musician should be taught to make this a definite matter of prayer. Each should ask the Lord to help him to communicate in the finest way possible. The total presentation should be done in a prayerful attitude, expecting the Holy Spirit to take up the slack and overcome inadequacies.

16

Music in Revivals

---

and Conferences

WHEREVER the gospel of Christ has been preached, churches have had "protracted meetings," "evangelistic campaigns," or more commonly, "revivals." Usually a great deal of evangelistic music accompanies these revivals. This music is largely geared to soul-winning, from congregational singing to solos. Scattered between would be special small ensembles, crusade choirs, and various types of instrumental music.

The real purpose for revival music is to prepare the hearts of the people for the soul-winning message of the evangelist, whether he be the pastor or a visiting speaker. Music has a profound effect on human beings; we see this in the popular music of our day, in the musical commercials on radio or television. Music has more of a mood-setting effect on some than on others. Preparing the minds and hearts of people attending the meetings can be done effectively, in the power of the Holy Spirit and with thought and planning.

132

The Music Director or Evangelistic Singer

Many churches have good music directors who can present an effective program of evangelistic music for a revival; and, in many cases, this is the best course to follow. In other cases, it is better to call in a special musician for the evangelistic campaign, for several reasons:

1. The church choir and musicians would have something new and different to look forward to. They would have the opportunity to sing or work with a guest musician. This adds interest for them and gives variety to the music program, just as a guest speaker provides a change in the pulpit. In other words, an evangelistic singer is brought in for the same reason a revivalist or guest speaker is brought in.

2. It gives the music director of the church, whether part-time or full-time, opportunity to share ideas with an outside musician and to work closely with him, thus offering the church a much better music program for the meetings.

3. It allows the evangelist more liberty in requesting the kind of music he feels necessary for his particular series of meetings.

The Revival Choir

In the regular church service the choir personnel must be made up of dedicated singers who are determined to remain faithful spring, summer, winter, and fall to the choir ministry. In an evangelistic campaign or Bible conference the choir can be augmented with persons who could not, for one reason or another, be faithful choir members all year. They can be a great help, because many faithful choir members have employment that requires them to work at night. Others can help the choir to be filled every evening. The regular, faithful choir members should be alerted to the relaxing of attendance rules, even for a short time.

If several churches have gone together for a meeting, the choir would be made up of singers from all the churches. Union campaigns can have great choirs, which are exciting to the people and thrilling for the individual participants.

Choice of Music

If new selections are used and only rehearsed each evening prior to the service or for a short period of time after the service, then the music must be kept relatively simple. Arrangements must be evangelistic for a revival meeting or inspiring for Bible conferences. Some music publishers are now preparing more simplified, more easily learned choir arrangements.

Because many evangelists like for the music program to lead into the sermon, consideration should be given to the subject to be dealt with each evening by the evangelist or the Bible conference speaker. This isn't always possible; many evangelists wait until they reach the platform for a final decision on what to preach. They have a storehouse of materials used in other places that they can depend on. A good evangelistic singer should not lose his composure in such a case, even though he is used to fitting his music program to the sermon subject. Any music director should have the ability to adapt himself to a particular situation and make the most of the opportunity presented to him.

Because of a limited amount of rehearsal time during revival meetings, the church music director, when he is in charge of the music, should depend on some of the more acceptable special numbers that have been presented in the last year or two. Revival meetings and conferences, which bring a lot of visitors to the services, are wonderful times to repeat gospel songs that have been a special blessing to past services.

Guest Singers

Although some pastors leave the total music program in the hands of their music director, they may invite special singers to come and help in the revival music program. A guest musician should be given some leeway to perform as he feels comfortable, yet an understanding should be reached before the meetings to assure total harmony during the evangelistic effort. It is not wise to invite a special singer or special music group without hearing them or having them recommended by one who understands your total music program and can assure you that they would fit in well.

The conversion experience and the Christian testimony of special singers, like the evangelist's, should be above reproach, because they are *ministers* in music during the Bible conference meeting. Plans for the sale of his records and books, the financial arrangements, and his entertainment during his stay should be taken care of before the guest singer arrives. Countless meetings have been hindered or even canceled because of a lack of understanding and proper communication before the meeting begins.

A guest musician will do well to remember that he is a *guest,* and should exhibit a spirit of cooperation and humility in the presence of the host music director and the host choir. He should be publicly complimentary toward them, whenever possible. He should be willing to help them in any way, especially if he is more experienced. Such opportunities of service should not be sought, but should be welcomed if they do appear.

Too often, guest singers tend to sing their "sugar sticks" during the Bible conference or evangelistic meeting. It is far better to prayerfully consider the needs of the people and to use songs that convey the message needed, even though they may not be best suited to the voice of the guest musician. The Lord will bless this approach far more than any other.

Instrumental Ensembles

Instrumental ensembles, well rehearsed and ready to perform, are a bright spot in any conference or protracted meeting. Any number of instrumental combinations may be used, but special meetings are not the time to throw them together. This should be done prior to the meeting, so that only the best possible performance is put before the people during the meetings. The instrumental ensemble should play familiar songs, easily recognizable to the people, as offertories, preludes, and postludes, just as the pianist and organist do. People mentally hear the lyrics as the music is played, so these presentations are a blessing to them. The message of the song, although not spoken or sung, is still presented by the instrumental ensemble; these songs should be presented as prayerfully and carefully as those that are sung.

Accompanists

One particular need in many churches is for good piano and organ accompanists. Although some churches cannot maintain a high caliber of accompanists throughout the year, they may invite guest accompanists to come for special meetings. These should be treated fairly in every way, financially, ethically, and spiritually. This requires adequate communication and planning before the meetings.

The guest accompanist should not assume the air of a celebrity coming in to show off his ability, but should remember that he is just "an accompanist," and do his utmost to stay in the background during the presentation of the music, with the possible exception of the offertories, preludes, and postludes. During the accompaniment for the choir or for guest musicians or singers, his attitude should be one of service and help. Never should he be guilty of playing a "solo" during the congregational singing, a choir special, or the presentation of a song by an individual or a group.

Guest accompanists should be tried and proved in their ability. They should have ability to sight-read very quickly. Much of the music that they will play will not be presented beforehand, so they must be able to play it readily.

Guest musicians will feel more welcome and play better if the instruments they are expected to play have been properly dusted and polished and, more than this, properly tuned before the meeting.

Songbooks

The regular hymnal is the proper songbook for a revival meeting in a church, but for a union campaign some attention should be given to having song sheets or special songbooks for the services. The evangelistic song leader should have the opportunity to choose the songs for the song sheets. This is usually considered a campaign expense cared for in the expense offerings.

It is best to have different song sheets each evening; if this is not possible, the song leader should be careful to have them collected each evening and reused; or new copies of the same song sheets may be furnished for the people as they enter the building each night. The song sheets need not have the full musical compositions, but just the words and possibly the "key" listed with each selection.

The Order of Service

The order of service should be determined by the host pastor; copies of cue cards should be given to all the principles—the host pastor, the visiting evangelist, the guest musician, the pianist, the organist, the head usher, and the operator of the public address system—prior to starting time each evening. The same order may be followed each evening, making it possible for the order of service to be mimeographed ahead of time; each evening the different musical selections can be inserted, along with the congregational songs. Many pastors want special meetings to be very flexible, and rightly so; but there needs to be some order to put the singers, accompanists, P.A. men, and ushers at ease. It can be kept in mind by all participating that there will be some flexibility in the order of service.

Invitation Song

The invitation song should be sung with fervor and a good rhythmic tempo, not be rushed or sung rapidly, but be lively.

It is often better to use only the choir during the invitation song, so that audience attention is not drawn away with thumbing hymnals to follow unfamiliar words. Their minds can be completely on the message they have heard, and on their need to make a decision.

The invitation song should be changed only by the pastor or guest evangelist. The music director should never take this upon himself, unless he is asked to do so by the pastor or evangelist in charge.

The song leader should never make finger signals to the accompanists near the close of the sermon or turn around and make gestures to the choir about the invitation song to be sung. With a little planning by the evangelist and song leader, such disturbances can be avoided. If the evangelist or pastor has not made a request for a particular invitation song, the song leader should have an appropriate number and title ready, so that it might be stated immediately, upon request, at the close of the sermon.

The accompanist should not play a long introduction for an invitation song; a simple chord is sufficient, so the choir and/or congregation know the starting pitch. A long introduction creates a "dead" spot and can distract the audience and the evangelist or pastor. This part of the service should run as smoothly as possible. The invitation time is a time for reaping. All the visitation, all the prayers, all the hours of study—the multiplied hours of work and concern on the part of many—are climaxed at this point. It is all-important that this portion of the service have complete and total priority.

17

Music, an Arm of Evangelism

MUSIC that cannot be considered a part of the total evangelistic outreach of the church should not be used in the church. There are so many ways that music can be an arm of evangelism in our churches.

The Sunday Services of the Church

Music that incorporates a message of salvation can cause people in the pews to literally yield their hearts to Christ on the spot. Recently, three couples yielded their heart and lives to Jesus Christ during the song service prior to the pastor's message. Many people, presently not living dedicated lives, were at one time faithful in church attendance. Thus, when they hear the great hymns and gospel songs sung during a church service, their hearts are strangely warmed and moved toward spiritual rededication or actual conversion: the message that follows is the clincher.

The Children's Choirs

Children's hearts are young and pliable and easily moved, especially through music. My two-year-old daughter has often learned more through the children's songs in the toddler's department of the Sunday school than from the spoken word, because these musical messages can be repeated at home, on the playground, or in her own bedroom at night. Family trips are often more cheerful because of songs that the children sing, which they learned in the children's choir.

There are some ways to reach children during the children's choir rehearsal that have nothing to do with the musical aspect of their meeting.

Devotional Time

Because the Beginner, Primary, and Junior choirs need several breaks during rehearsal, a devotional period can be used effectively. During this devotional period several practical lessons can be taught, and the plan of salvation can be presented periodically. On several occasions the author has presented the play of salvation in the children's choir. Those who were interested in learning how to be saved remained after the others had gone, when more time was available for counseling. But the first contact with them was made during the devotional time of the children's choir.

Visits in the Home

A dedicated children's choir director has a perfect entrance into the home of a choir member. Imagine the choir director walking up to the front door of a home, knocking, and when the mother answers the door, saying, "I am Mrs. Smith, director of the Primary Choir at First Baptist Church. Your son, Johnny, is in my choir, and he is such a fine boy I wanted to come and meet his parents. Are you Mrs. Jones?" The director would not be denied entrance into one out of ten thousand homes that she approached with that attitude. Even though the parents may already be Christians, she can invite them to the services, and they may become church members because their little boy became a member of a children's choir at the church.

Music Draws New People

At the Northwest Baptist Church, Miami, Florida, whole families have joined the church because of the teen choir that sang every Sunday morning there. Adults want their teens to be engaged in the activities of the church. Such participation assures parents that the young lives will be pointed in the right direction. A large teen choir can attract not only parents, but other teens as well.

Juniors like to be a part of the mass; a large Junior choir attracts Junior-age children. This is also true of Primaries and Beginners.

Choir directors of large, effective adult choirs are often approached by people who say, "I just had to come back and hear your fine music program." Some people respond to music as to no other Christian activity.

Services in Other Locations

There are numerous opportunities for church musicians to be of service to Christ outside the church services. They may be asked, or may ask, to sing in rest homes or jails.

Many forgotten souls are housed in the numerous rest homes of virtually every city in America. Their spirits can be lifted to great heights with your music.

The prisons are an ever-increasing mission field. The inmates have all had some appreciation for music in the outside world. Share your musical testimony with them. In most cases, the wardens will be delighted to arrange your visit.

Choir tours are very popular these days.

These opportunities for appearing at special civic affairs are too numerous to mention. Some are (1) state legislature houses; (2) civic club meetings; (3) shopping centers; (4) street or park open-air services; or (5) home meetings, and the list could go on and on.

18

Congregational Singing

and Song Leading

IF music directors, universally, have a single weakness, it is in congregational song leading. It seems to require a particular talent that is either inherent or developed, and the importance of which cannot be overstressed. Good congregational song leading has accompanied every spiritual awakening in every major revival, in which many hundreds, or even thousands, have come to know Christ as Savior. Congregational singing led by the organist is not enough. A dominant personality needs to be on the platform in complete control and command of the situation.

The real purpose of the song service is to lead the congregation in the real Christian experience of singing praises to God and communicating with him through song. The audience will enter in with more enthusiasm, and will receive more from the song service, if it is led by an outstanding song leader.

Everyone should be able to see a hymnal, even if he must share one with his neighbor. The congregational song leader should make sure that the hymnals or songbooks are evenly distributed throughout the congregation, so that all may participate in the singing.

Several aspects of congregational song leading need to be considered.

The Selection of Songs

Songs should not be selected at the last moment, or chosen lightly or according to whims or personal likes. The particular service in which they are to be used should be taken into consideration.

1. The Sunday morning service has been for many years, thought of as a worship service by most congregational song leaders and pastors. The congregational singing must, therefore, be worshipful, with songs of praise. Instead, since this is the time when more lost people are in the congregation, this service should be evangelistic. Songs for Sunday morning should have a gospel message.

Since pastors do not usually announce their subjects prior to the morning service, the music director cannot plan around a particular theme. He should, then, give more consideration to bringing the minds and hearts of the people into focus by his choice of good gospel songs.

2. The Sunday evening service is a time when the song leader can broaden out and use songs that are not necessarily evangelistic, but are good gospel songs, helpful to any congregation. This does not exclude songs with a message of salvation, because many Sunday evening services are soul-winning services. But, by and large, the Sunday evening service lends itself to a large variety of music.

3. The Wednesday service offers an opportunity for some other congregational songs to be used. For the most part, only the church family is present, and, therefore, light, happy songs may be used, at least during part of the service.

The song leader must, at all times, keep his congregation in mind, being constantly aware of the individuals making up the congregation. Some congregations are made up of more highly educated persons than others. Some are rural in nature. The song leader should take into consideration the majority of the congregation and be practical in his selection of congregational songs. However, a more educated congregation would occasionally enjoy the simple, light, lilting songs, just as the rural or less educated congregation would enjoy the more serious hymns.

Congregations also differ vastly geographically. In many sections of the South songs of the "Southern quartet convention" type have been used for so long that a song leader would find it difficult to plan service after service without including some songs of this nature. These should be sung strictly according to the timing indicated in the book, and be done in good taste always.

In reverse, many congregations, who have never been exposed to this kind of singing, would be greatly offended if it were introduced into their congregational singing.

Platform Personality

Song leaders must keep one thing in mind: they are not preaching, but preparing the people for the sermon. Often a Scripture passage or a poem comes to mind, and a great deal of time is used in exhortations between songs or even between stanzas of a song. Lengthy ad-libbing is usually not welcomed by the pastor or evangelist who is about to speak. The song leader should have some freedom to make statements to enhance the song service, but his talking should be limited.

The song leader should announce the number of each song clearly and distinctly and with sufficient volume so that those in the back might hear easily, even without a public address system. The number should then be repeated once or twice, so that everyone knows exactly what song is to be sung.

The song leader, when not leading the singing, should pay close attention to all that is being said in the pulpit. Signals or whispers to the choir or the accompanists during the announcements or the offering should be minimal. Occasionally these may be necessary but, for the most part, should be avoided.

The song leader should sit erect on the platform, with legs crossed loosely at the knee, if at all, avoiding any distraction of the congregation by unnecessary movement or unusual position.

The song leader should watch the pastor closely as he speaks, with only an occasional glance out over the audience to see that everything is in order.

Use of Hymn Stories

For nearly twenty years I have studied hymnology and found the subject most interesting. On many occasions I have used hymn stories in public services to great advantage. Many books giving the stories behind the hymns are on the market today, most of them fairly accurate. These stories usually have great human interest. Many songs were born of dark, trying times in the lives of the composers. Everyone likes a story; therefore, interest in the song service can be spurred with the wise use of a hymn story. The following guidelines may be helpful.

1. Some hymn stories, although widely circulated, have not a shred of truth and should be avoided. How can God bless a lie? Stories from reputable books should be used, for their accuracy can usually be depended on.

Never choose a congregational song that is not appropriate to the occasion just because the story behind the song is a tear-jerker. Hymn stories should be carefully chosen with prayer and a sincere desire to augment the service with its use.

Stories behind good singable congregational songs, and occasionally stories behind gospel songs used as solos, may be used; but solo songs should never be used as congregational number, if they do not lend themselves to group singing.

2. Use only one hymn story in a particular service, unless the occasion demands more. In a Bible conference or a series of evangelistic meetings, a guest singer might use one each night to great advantage, but ordinarily it is never advisable to use one at every service, or even once a week. To keep the technique fresh and unusual, it is advisable to use only one each month or two.

Most major publishers of Christian literature have at least one book of hymn stories. If your town has a Christian bookstore, the proprietor may stock hymn stories, or if not, he can put you in touch with companies that can furnish them. Following is a list of books of hymn stories and their publishers, which, while not exhaustive, will give you an idea of some things you can use.

Great Hymns of Their Stories
  Christian Literature Crusade
  Fort Washington, Pennsylvania

Forty Gospel Hymn Stories
  The Rodeheaver-Hall Mack Co.
  Winona Lake, Indiana

Lyric Religion
  Fleming H. Revell Co.
  New York, New York

Famous Stories of Inspiring Hymns
  W. A. Wilde Co. Publishers
  Boston, Massachusetts

Stories of Fadeless Hymns
  Broadman Press
  Nashville, Tennessee

In Every Corner Sing
  Muhlenburg Press
  Philadelphia, Pennsylvania

One Hundred and One Hymn Stories
  Abingdon Press
  Nashville, Tennessee

A Hymn Is Born
  Broadman Press
  Nashville, Tennessee

The Story of the Hymns and Tunes
  Zondervan Publishing House
  Grand Rapids, Michigan

Good Morning, Lord!
  Baker Book House
  Grand Rapids, Michigan

Dr. J. R. Faulkner, the co-pastor of Highland Park Baptist Church, Chattanooga, Tennessee, has led the congregational singing in that great church for many years. He has learned to handle audiences as few other leaders have. On the following pages he shares his ideas concerning this important aspect of the church services.

EFFECTIVE CONGREGATIONAL SINGING

by J. R. Faulkner

I am frank to state that, in my opinion, congregational singing would take the Number 2 place in the ministry of the Word, but it is essential to an effective ministry. It is true that congregational singing has a ministry within itself, because it conveys the great truths of the Word of God. It also has a therapeutic value for the people. It quiets their minds and hearts and brings them into an attitude of worship, preparing them to receive the truth of God's Word as it is delivered by the minister later in the service. I do not think that the music should ever take the place of the preaching of the Word of God, but it should be a handmaiden to revival and to an effective Bible ministry.

Happy is the songleader who has a well-trained organist and pianist who pay attention to him as he opens the service. I have been well blessed in this regard through all the years of my ministry at Highland Park Baptist Church. Mrs. Charles Harris and Mrs. Fred Brown have been our accompanists. They are quick to note the simple gesture that is the signal to begin. I may never look at the organist after bringing the people to their feet, but a simple motion with my left hand brings her into the accompaniment. I ask our accompanists to always play the first phrase of the song for an introduction. This brings to mind the words of the first verse and makes it easier for the people to begin with me. I never encourage a long introduction; just an opening measure or two is sufficient.

When announcing a song, I give the number first, and then I make a brief comment about the song or give a word of encouragement to the people to join with us as we sing. I always repeat the number of the song for those who are slow listeners and do not get it the first time. They will be thumbing through the index, so I repeat the number at the close of my comment.

There are certain unwritten rules that I follow in selecting songs and hymns for the service. I begin with one that is well known and very singable. If I plan to use a hymn that is lesser known, I present it as the second or third song in the format. I try to follow the theme established by the pastor in his message, if possible. If not, I concentrate on instilling the proper attitude into the people so that they are ready for the message, whatever it might be. Since our pastor is a musician and loves for people to sing vigorously, I choose at least one song in our evening services that leads to a dramatic ending. Notable examples are "One Day" and "Heaven Came Down and Glory Filled My Soul." There are many others in our better hymnals. If I am bringing the service to a prayer time, I try to use songs with a stilling effect to induce a more worshipful spirit. I give the service to the pastor in a lowered tone. On the other hand, if announcements or offering are next, I end my part of the song service on a high, inspirational tone.

In choosing songs I try to remember the key signatures as well as the time signatures. I think this adds variety to the song service and makes for more enthusiastic singing.

The size of the conducting pattern is regulated by the size of the audience. At the Highland Park Baptist Church I'm leading 2,000 to 3,500 people in an average congregation, and, naturally, I work with arms at full length. We have an unusually large balcony and a large main floor. In order to be seen, I try to follow a pattern rigidly, and I try to work it at arm's length so that I may be seen by all.

I avoid repeating ordinary songs within a thirty-day period. I keep a record of every song used and how many times it has been used in our services; even the use of gospel choruses is recorded. I can check with my secretary to find out how many times we have used any song within the past six to twelve months. I have an old hymnal that I use to prepare my song services. I make a pencil notation in the margin of the book as to when I last used each song. I even keep a notation of the songs used by visiting musicians.

I do not dominate the pulpit until my pastor is present. For instance, in opening the morning service, for years I did not sit down on the platform until my pastor put in his appearance.

If I chose to sit down, I sat in one of the chairs by the piano or organ and waited until my pastor approached. Prior to this, I would have checked the PA system, the organ, and all the electronic equipment we use. I would check the building for lights or for any problems relating to the ushering. These things are checked thirty to forty-five minutes before every regular service. If I have the responsibility of being in the pulpit prior to my pastor's appearance—and occasionally I do—when he appears I immediately stand and wait until he is seated. Our choir is then brought in at the given moment with an organ accompaniment. They remain standing till all are in position. We have the opening number by the choir, and then I turn to the audience to begin the congregational singing.

19

Cantatas

FOR many years one of the integral parts of church music has been the presentation of cantatas. There are many different kinds of cantatas, but most often they are used at Christmas. Cantatas are also performed at Easter; and there are, of late, missionary cantatas appropriate for other times. Cantatas have advanced technically, so that learning and presenting them has become much more interesting and exciting to both performers and hearers.

For too many years, Sunday evening services have been abused by the use of cantatas. Some may debate this, but it has long been my belief that the Sunday evening service should be used as every other service—for the preaching of the gospel. It is not necessarily wrong for a cantata to take the place of the preaching service, just unwise. Many churches have lost in attendance on a particular night because people wanted to hear a gospel sermon. It is also true that people would attend an evening preaching service who would not come for a cantata.

The following ideas have been formed over many years of presenting cantatas.

Benefits Derived from Cantatas

Those who have composed cantatas have, through the years, made a great contribution to church music and have been greatly helpful to many people. Cantatas are of special benefit to the following:

1. *The church benefits.* Many composers spend hours in prayer and hard labor, and the resulting music is a very moving, spiritual experience for a church as they listen to a cantata. A great deal of effort is required for the composer to link together the music and the message so that the deep spiritual meanings are not lost but are enhanced by the musical setting.

It is up to the music director not to abuse the use of cantatas, but to use them in a way that that will cause the church to be helped and not hindered by his presentation of them.

2. *The choir can be helped in several ways by the presentation of cantatas.* As in any other project a group of people who have trained long and hard gain a great sense of accomplishment with the finished, presented work. Each member feels that he has been a part of something grand and glorious, if the cantata is presented well and in a professional manner. This lifting of the spirits carries over into the regular church service performance and causes the choir to be better both musically and spiritually.

The choir is helped musically. Often a composer is able to challenge the more highly trained choir and, at the same time, allow the lesser trained choirs to perform, because he has provided a variety of music.

Long hours are spent rehearsing cantatas; and drilling and rehearsing help to develop the choir musically. The difficult passages help them to have a better "musical" ear, thus enabling them to perform all their music in a better way. Cantatas usually require extra rehearsals; but most choir members do not mind spending three or four extra evenings in preparation for a Christmas or Easter musical.

Cantatas also help the choir to watch the conductor. A heretofore unfamiliar musical composition demands of them the very best that they can muster in the last rehearsals and in the performance.

3. *The choir seems to become more closely knit together*. At no other time is the personnel of a choir drawn together in one heart and one spirit more than during the preparation for a cantata. This may not be true of all choirs, but it seems to be true of most.

4. *Individual choir members also are benefitted by cantatas*. No Choir ever reaches its greatest potential until individual members see themselves as part of the choir. This sounds paradoxical, since a choir is supposed to act as one unit, with all individuals in the whole acting together. Each individual must be cognizant of the fact that the choir is made up of individuals like himself, and the choir is only as faithful as he is. The choir concentrates as individuals concentrate. The choir learns as individuals learn. The choir takes pride in performance as individuals take pride in performance. All of this can be greatly enhanced by the rehearsal and presentation of a cantata. A cantata is not the complete answer, but it helps individual choir members.

Rapid Mastery of Cantatas

One of the almost insurmountable obstacles in good choir performance is the lack of time people seem to have. It is increasingly difficult to capture the minds and the attention of large numbers of people for enough rehearsal periods to make a good performance.

A few years ago I discovered a wonderful way to cut, almost by two thirds, the amount of rehearsal time necessary for a choir to present a good musical. Let me share my discovery with you.

Procedure

Individual choir members, if they have their personal copies of the cantata score plus a recording of it, can sit down at home, play the record, follow the score, and learn the cantata in its entirety.

When they go into rehearsal, they are so familiar with the overall score, and even with their individual parts, that they are able to join in the rehearsal with enthusiasm and knowledge, making it very simple for the choir to master the score in record time.

The time saved in this manner, which is usually spent in sectional rehearsals on individual parts, can be used to polish the overall performance and give more attention to releases and to dynamics indicated in the score.

This method of learning a cantata uses the cantata "kit." Advancements in recording technology make it possible for publishing houses to produce most cantatas in kit form. In each kit is a long-play record album of the cantata, plus a score and samples of advertising materials, bulletins, etc. The cost of the kits is nominal, making it inexpensive for each member of the choir to own his personal kit. Kits were originally designed for directors, so that they might use the recording to learn the cantata easily and teach it to the choir more rapidly. Carrying this a step further, as has been suggested, can cut rehearsal time by as much as two thirds.

Cantata kits may be ordered from the publisher in quantities and, in some cases, at a discount. Even more classical musicals that are not in kit form are available on long-play record albums at a nominal cost.

Results

The most important result obtained from using the kits is that the choir feels much more effective in the church services just before and immediately after the performance of the cantata, because they have been able to spend more time working on music for the scheduled services. Cantatas should be avoided, if the services are going to be hindered or harmed in any way because of an ineffective choir.

When a choir is using the cantata kits, only a few minutes spent on the cantata in several rehearsals prior to the time of performance will be adequate. Otherwise, the choir must be willing to spend three or four nights over and above their regular rehearsal time to prepare for the cantata.

It is effective to present in the services prior to the performance date a few parts from the cantata. This whets the appetite of the audience for the entire performance.

Scheduling Cantatas

This is left up to the individual pastor and music director, but it is strongly suggested that musical presentations not supersede or replace a regular preaching service. They should be given in addition to the sermon, or—and this is preferable—on a separate night or Sunday afternoon.

The advantages to this are several.

1. It leaves the services intact to reach the lost for Christ.
2. A cantata performance on Sunday afternoon or a week night allows members of other churches to attend and still remain faithful to their own services.
3. It also lets the people of the congregation know that the pastor, the music director, and the members of the choir feel that the church services are important and that the preaching of the gospel is the most important thing.

Cantata Selection

Each year several new cantatas or musicals are published by major publishing companies. A great deal of exciting patriotic material is published. The Fourth of July or midsummer cantatas are very appropriate. These are especially good for teen ensembles. There are also many missionary cantatas that may be done at almost any time of the year.

It is easy for a music director to stay within the circle of a very few favorite musical scores, but he should broaden out, seeking newer and better material so as to give his choir a knowledge of the best available music.

The ability of the choir regulates the selection of the cantatas.

Some scores are less difficult than others, and a choir director must give this consideration in choosing a work for his choir. It is far better for a choir to do a cantata beneath their capability, than for them to tackle a too-difficult musical score with the limited rehearsal that is usually possible. Nothing sounds worse than an otherwise beautiful composition botched up because it is over the heads of the performers. Keep the music within reach of the performers.

The content of the material or the message that is proclaimed is of great importance also. The selection should be read through for Scriptural content and doctrinal accuracy. The fact that the composer has done a good job musically does not always constitute reason enough to perform a work.

Additional Accompaniment

Some churches are fortunate enough to have outstanding musicians as members of the congregation. These musicians, whether violinists, trumpet players, saxophonists, clarinetists, etc., may be used. Local band directors or school musicians may be able to help in writing some accompaniment if you cannot do so. Some cantatas are available with orchestration.

This additional accompaniment allows those who play instruments, and have spent years developing this talent, an opportunity to be used in the church music and to be part of an outstanding musical presentation.

If only one or two instruments are available, there are several ways they might be used; this is up to the director and his imagination. A local band director may be helpful in making suggestions. Inviting his ideas along this line is good for public relations and may give an opportunity to win him to Christ if he is not a Christian.

20

Christian Music

in the Home

NO place in the world should be happier than our homes. Where there is happiness, there is always singing; therefore, a great deal of singing is done in a happy home, perhaps more in some than in others, but always singing. Fortunate indeed are children born to parents who love singing and are musically inclined. This does not mean that parents who are not musical cannot recognize the need for music and provide music opportunities for their children.

There are many aspects of music in the home but the music to be discussed in this chapter is the music learned at church and carried over into the home, and the music learned at home and carried into the church. There are many ways that music can be a great asset to the home.

Many men, in their later years, are reminded of their childhood training in the home at a mother's knee, through hearing a song that brought back golden memories. Singing indelibly imprints the blessings of God and Christian doctrines in the minds of young children. My two children (ages two and four) first exhibited knowledge of Christian teachings through the songs learned in Sunday school classes. Children bring songs into the home, and the songs are learned and shared in happy home situations. The singing or home musical participation need not even be of high caliber from a musical standpoint, but it can be an effective tool in the hands of Christian parents.

Total Participation

Whether in the family altar or in other home situations, all the family should be encouraged to participate in the music in the home. Each child should share equally in musical training opportunities; if music lessons are extended to one, they should be given to all who are old enough. Older children who did not have the opportunity for music training may encourage younger brothers and sisters to take advantage of present opportunities. Every member of the family should be exposed to Christian music, whether in family songfests, music lessons, sacred recordings, or attendance at musical concerts.

Family singing can be carried on at various times when all can naturally and freely sing together.

At Devotions

After Scripture reading and prayer, all the family may sing together a hymn or a chorus that one of the children has learned and loves. To link a Christian doctrine to a melody is to cement it in the mind, because one can go about humming the tune while the words play through the mind. He is thus repeating the lessons learned in the family devotional time.

Good Morning, Lord is a book of family devotions I have written. It suggests that, after the Scripture passage is read and a favorite verse memorized, the story behind a famous Christian song be used as a devotional thought. After this lesson is learned and the hymn history tucked away into the minds, the family may sing the song around the family altar. After this, a devotional thought may close the devotional period. Use of Christian songs and choruses in your family devotions is highly recommended.

On Automobile Trips

Some of my family's most delightful times were spent riding along together, singing wonderful gospel choruses and songs, including those the children were learning in Sunday school. As these were repeated over and over, they were learned well and joined the repertoire. Over the miles, another and another was learned, until the family could sing together a great many songs.

Singing in the car does not have to be reserved for vacation or extended trips; you can sing on short trips to church and back or on a shopping spree. There may be times when singing just does not seem to be in order; but there are other times when it seems the only thing to do. Some fathers and mothers say, "I can't carry a tune in a bucket." They should forget that bit of nonsense and join the songs, even though they may sing every note on the same pitch. The idea is to enter into the joy and spirit of the occasion, not to become a part of a great musical production.

At Family Get-Togethers or Reunions

Nothing seems to please grandparents quite so much as the singing of their grandchildren. Therefore, the children should be encouraged to join in a little songfest while visiting grandma and grandpa. The time spent around the piano singing the songs of the church will be golden memories in years to come. This is not always possible because of the lack of a piano or someone to play the piano. But whenever possible, such singing should be engaged in with joy.

Children's Choir Home Study

Very often parents have the opportunity and privilege of helping their children with music—or words—to be learned at home. Often the children's choir director will duplicate the lyrics and send them home with the children, asking the parents to help the children learn the words to the song being used in the choir. (This should only be done if the music is public domain.) Rehearsal time being at a minimum, the choir directors need all the help they can get with teaching the music. This is one way that parents can feel they are helping and participating in church music with their children. Parents should make sure that children learn their choir songs, just as they make sure that they prepare their lessons each day for the secular school.

Music Lessons

Many families are so hard-pressed financially that it is almost impossible for their children to take private music lessons. Today, with the great advancement in music study in the public schools, many children, who could not otherwise afford it, may be able to have some music instruction. Parents should make sure that their children take advantage of every opportunity, so they can serve Christ well when they grow into young men and women. If the school furnishes instruments and free lessons, these should be utilized.

Pianos and musical instruments (such as organs) are very costly, and comparatively few can afford them. Those who can should encourage their children to appreciate the opportunity of music lessons and to apply themselves to practice.

There are many kinds of music lessons available for young people.

1. Voice lessons for a child of nine, ten, or eleven years of age are, in most cases, a waste of money and time. Children—boys always, and girls, in most cases—should wait until they are fifteen or sixteen years of age to study voice privately, because the voice change should have settled into some definite category before this extensive period of private instruction begins. A person can learn some of the basic fundamentals, such as breathing exercises and techniques and voice placement prior to that age, but these things may be learned very quickly after serious voice training has begun at age fifteen to seventeen. It takes about five years of weekly private instructions and daily vocal and breathing exercises to harden the abdominal muscles and bring the whole vocal mechanism into proper maturity. There is no short-cut, no quick

method. Some youth are more talented in the beginning than others, but even those with greater talent may not reach the heights they are capable of if they cut their training short.

2. Piano lessons are another "advantage" in which many parents make a serious mistake by starting children too early. This has been discussed in an earlier chapter, so little will be said here on that subject.

Young children who learn the basic keyboard are headed in the right direction for serious music training, because all music stems from the concert key, which is the piano keyboard. It would be greatly beneficial for young people who plan to study any type of instrument to know something about the piano keyboard. Most great composers, conductors, and arrangers are excellent pianists. Most good orchestrations are done right at the piano keyboard. The piano is a most versatile instrument. Some people have a knack for playing the piano, while other must engage in a long and tedious struggle to master this grand instrument. Some seem almost to be born with the ability to play it. This is one of the great musical mysteries.

An ability to play the piano well yields many opportunities of Christian service: church services, revival meetings, Bible conferences, Sunday school classes and departments—the list could go on and on.

3. All the various musical instruments for which private instruction is available are too numerous to mention here, but they range from the piccolo to the tuba, from the guitar to the harmonica. A child who shows a flair or unusual interest in a particular instrument is more likely to excel in that instrument—that is, if his character is developed to the point that he can stick with the instrument long enough to become proficient.

Children raised in rural areas may not have as great a choice of instruments as those in cities will have. But children everywhere have some opportunities and should avail themselves of those open doors as they are presented.

4. In music study, as in many other areas of a child's life, the parents must guide them in deciding what is right or wrong, or what is to be done at a particular time. Often children begin

taking private music lessons and are very excited for a brief period of time, but eventually the "new" wears off. Practice becomes a drudgery and a chore. Unfortunately, this is not only true in young children, but also in teenagers and adults. To allow a child to take up something new, be enthusiastic awhile, and then drop it before long is greatly detrimental to the character development of the child. Tremendous talent may be lost and go completely unrecognized by the parents, simply because they did not insist that the child stick with what he had started.

Young, immature minds cannot see the end from the beginning and therefore are not capable of seeing the value of hours of rehearsal. They may have seen someone who plays an instrument well and considered only the exciting, romantic aspect of their performance that appears on the surface. If children are forced to continue in what they have started, they will learn a lesson in perseverance. They need not continue indefinitely, but they should keep up their commitment to the project until they and the parents see that it is useless to continue.

The greatest men of history seem to have learned early to sit down with their counselors, chart a course, determine which is the right direction, and then pursue that course. Though they ran into insurmountable difficulties on many occasions, they were not deterred from their plans; nor would they give in.

In a child's instrumental practice, time becomes a factor; school lessons become a factor; the family schedule becomes a factor; many other things too numerous to mention enter into the picture. These difficulties need to be worked out, not because you are trying to train a great musician, but because you are trying to teach a child a lesson that will be valuable to him in life in many, many other situations.

Perfect Pitch

Many musicians have what is commonly known as "perfect" or "absolute" pitch. This simply means that they are able to name a particular note after hearing it played, even though they cannot see which key is being played. They can hear a note sung by another person and tell exactly what pitch it is, or they can start singing a song in a particular key without having heard any note or pitch given on an instrument. The reason for mentioning this here is that a child's perfect pitch may be recognized in the home by an older brother or sister, or by a parent with musical ability.

Such was the case of Beverly Hahn, of Tampa, Florida. About 1938, when Beverly was only four years of age, her father, a musician of some reputation, was doing some yardwork when Beverly ran up to him and cried, "Daddy, Daddy, that train blew a G!" He turned to her and said, "What did you say?" and she repeated, "That train just blew a G!" He asked her to explain, and she said that when the passing train blew its whistle, the whistle sounded the same as the G on the piano. He quickly ran into the house and to the piano, waiting for the train to blow the whistle again. Sure enough, when it did, he hit G on the piano and the pitch was identical. He called Beverly into the house and asked her to stand across the room, looking away from the piano. He carefully sounded note after note, asking her to name them. She named all of them correctly, so he discovered that she had perfect pitch.

Beverly received good musical training, and when she was eighteen, she went away to Tennessee Temple College in Chattanooga, Tennessee, and subsequently joined the Highland Park Baptist Church. The evening that she presented herself to the church for membership the pastor, Dr. Lee Roberson (without previously discussing his plan with her) decided to teach his congregation a lesson, even though his sermon had already closed. He announced to his congregation that Miss Hahn had absolute pitch and asked the organist to sound a note on the organ. He then asked Beverly to name the note. She immediately responded, "That's A sharp." He then asked the organist to sound another note, and Beverly named it correctly. He turned to the congregation and said, "Don't tell me that you don't believe in God, because only God can give that ability to a human being."

All parents would not be in position to recognize this extreme musical talent in a child, as was Mr. Hahn. But they can recognize some musical bent. Through competent counseling, they can obtain help in guiding a child toward a possible musical career or sufficient music training to make him a more useful servant of God, better able to enjoy the finer things in life and participate in the church music program.

How Family Music Helps the Church

While all the varied details of this subject cannot be discussed, we can say that, in a very real sense, the music programs in our churches would be but a fraction of their present size if it were not for music in the homes. This takes in private music lessons for some children, singing around the family altar and on automobile trips, family encouragement of children entering into school and church music activities, and the willingness of parents to finance family music projects.

Many of our adult choirs are what they are, because years ago parents saw the need to train their children musically, and these children in turn have become adults and are in strategic places in the choir, leading those with less music training. Church music would be crippled if it were not for homes that encourage participation in music.

21

Music and the

Church Budget

A GOOD church music program costs money, a lot of money. Some churches think that whatever the music program costs, it is inexpensive compared to the tremendous results. When the church decides that they are willing to make some expenditures for the music program, the program is on its way to becoming an integral part of the church ministry. For too many years, the average church member has felt that the music program is something "scratched together" on Sunday morning, with little preparation, and that operates at no cost other than the price of the piano or the organ. Pianos, organs, and music supplies have, as have all commodities, experienced inflation. It takes more money now than it did a few years ago to have a good music program.

If, in fact, the music budget is planned, it must deal with several questions.

Why Have a Music Budget?

The Scriptures exhort that "all things should be done decently and in order." The word "all" is inclusive and covers the music program. If money is going to be spent on the music program, it should be spent in an orderly manner with a budget. The music director or someone in charge should help to determine how much is actually needed for music over a twelve-month period. If a budget is being drawn up for the first time, then wise counsel should be sought from pastors and music directors who have done such planning for several years.

A budget will force a choir director to plan his music expenditures and be able to give reasons for the purchases. No music director should be given unlimited purchasing power, because this is a temptation to overspend and waste God's money. Every human being needs to answer to somebody for his actions; therefore, a budget ensures that the music director or the purchasing agent for the music department will exercise proper caution in spending the money.

A church budget will keep the expenditures for music in line with expenditures for other things in the music program. While it is sad to spend an excessive amount, it is even sadder to take short-cuts and cause the total church program to suffer.

What Does the Money Buy?

1. Sheet music is a valid category for the music budget. Most good, new compositions are published in sheet music form, and three copies of a single title (one for the soloist, one for the organist, and one for the pianist) will cost about $4.50, as opposed to $1.50 a few years ago. In the course of a year, it is easy to see what 45 or 50 selections would cost.

2. Collections of choir arrangements range in price from $1.00 to $1.95. The number of selections in a book will vary from eight to fifteen or twenty. The books with a larger number of selections are usually expensive, with more pages but, in some cases, simpler arrangements. By adding one collection of choir arrangements every month or two, quite a volume of choir music can be collected over a year's time.

These books have a way of disappearing and should be carefully guarded by the choir librarian.

3. The tuning and repair of pianos and organs are budget expenses. All pianos, no matter how expensive or inexpensive, get out of tune—new pianos more quickly than older ones. Environment has a great deal to do with the piano's ability to stay in tune. Continual changes of temperature cause the piano to need tuning often. For instance, a piano kept in an air-conditioned room needs tuning more often than one in a room with a constant temperature.

Tuning of pianos costs more in recent years, so that a large church with several pianos can have a sizable tuning and repair bill; therefore, these costs need to be covered in the church music budget.

Some choir directors have learned to tune the pianos themselves. This is a great advantage, because piano tuners are not always available when they are needed. A director with ability and tools can tune the pianos as often as necessary to keep them perfectly in tune, with only the expense of the tools and his time.

4. Music folders are needed for the choir. The best music folder this writer has found can be obtained from the Clamp Back Organization, 30 15th Avenue, North Hopkins, Minnesota. A little more expensive than the usual choir folder, they are worth more because they last much longer. They range in price from about $2.00 to $2.35, according to specifications. Therefore, a large choir can have a sizable folder cost that also needs to be included in the church music budget.

5. Files for choir music are needed. There are many different kinds of choir music files—some for the octavo size and some for the regular $8 \frac{1}{2} \times 11$ music. The number of files needed depends on the amount of sheet music used, so this expense may vary.

6. Single choir arrangements are a good investment. Many companies now publish singly some favorite arrangements from choir collections. These may be purchased at prices from 15 to 30 cents per copy.

7. Robes or special clothing may be a budget item. New robes for a choir are not always but may be worked into the annual budget. Many choirs dress the ladies in matching dresses and

the men in matching ties and blazers, as opposed to robes. Often these special outfits are worn only on special occasions. These are not usually in the church budget but are paid for by the choir members. At least one choir—the Adult Choir of the Northside Baptist Church, in Charlotte, North Carolina, that I presently direct—collects monthly gifts from each choir member for the purpose of buying special clothing.

A great deal of money can be saved by buying robe "kits." These are robes that are not sewn together. They are cut out, and come with all of the incidentals that will be needed for sewing the robes together. The members of the church or choir sew them together. This amounts to considerable savings to the church.

Some churches go even further and get patterns and materials and make robes from scratch. If the tailoring is done carefully, the robes look as nice and as costly as robes that are purchased ready-made.

8. Revivals and conferences cost money. Although music for revivals is often favorite songs and choir arrangements previously used in the church, there are some occasions when special expenses must be incurred for music for revivals and special meetings. There may be some additional duplicating or music purchasing to be done: these things must come out of a music budget.

9. Miscellaneous expenses can include: (1) chorus sheets and songbooks for Sunday school departments; (2) music staff stencils for duplicating; (3) flash cards and other visual aids for music training during the choir rehearsal.

How are Budget Amounts Determined?

The vision of some churches is greater than others, and they would therefore use more money for the music program. But there is a rule of thumb that can be used by most churches to determine an equitable and fair amount for the music budget. When a church has a budget of $50,000 annually or less, music expenditures need to be kept small. A smaller church needs to keep a good music program going as well as a larger church, but it is much more difficult for smaller churches to have the financial liberty to pursue a large music program.

With $50,000 or above as annual figures, sizable amounts of money can be taken without damaging the total effectiveness of the church. This writer feels that of an annual church budget of $50,000, 1 percent of that amount should be spent each year for the music program. This means that a church with a $50,000 budget would spend $500 in the music program; consequently, a church with $500,000 each year would spend $5,000 per year on the music budget. That seems like an enormous figure, but, compared to the total budget, it is minutely fractional.

How Can a Church Conserve Expenditures?

Every music director should consider himself a dedicated servant of Christ and realize that the music budget comes from offerings given by the rank and file of the church membership, the tithes and offerings of children, teenagers, and adults. This money should be used wisely and prayerfully, so that the maximum effectiveness can be gained from a minimum amount of financial expenditure. This means that, occasionally, the director will make his own choir arrangement of a song instead of buying a collection of choir arrangements at $1.95 each, to get one popular or favorite arrangement. This also means that the music director will supervise those working with him in the music program (accompanists and children's choir workers), and guide their purchases of music and materials, to be sure that the funds are conserved as much as possible.

22

Caring for the Piano

and Organ

THIS chapter is not written to give technical information, but to review some of the more practical aspects of caring for the musical instruments for any lay person who has charge of this phase of the church's music program.

Everyone knows the piano and the organ are intricate, costly instruments; therefore, it is a terrible waste of the Lord's money to improperly care for them. The proper care can be divided into six categories.

Proper Tuning

Every piano needs to be checked periodically for proper sound. An organ (especially later models) never needs tuning; their tuning is locked in at the factory with the exclusive lock-in systems that many organ companies possess. Pitch, however, can be adjusted to match the other instruments, if necessary. Any reputable organ repairman can adjust this in a few minutes.

The piano is quite a different story and is therefore considered in more detail. There are two types of tuning for the piano.

Manual Tuning

This old standby method is relied on by many outstanding musicians and orchestra conductors as being most effective. The tuner takes a tuning fork to tune A above Middle C and builds the whole tuning job from that point. Really adept piano tuners have musical ears, plus years of experience in hearing relative pitches correctly. Tuning an instrument, in need of no other repairs, takes only a short time for a good tuner.

All new pianos are tuned at the factory, but some dealers tune them after placing them on display in the store. They should be checked again for proper tuning after purchase and delivery. If they are fairly well in tune, after about two months of use, they should be given a "hard tuning." This is done by pounding briskly on each note as the tuner goes up and down the keyboard tuning each string. New pianos tend to loose their tune very quickly, because the new strings stretch more readily. The tautness of piano strings causes them to keep proper pitch. Upon examining the strings, you will find the lower keys have only one string, the keys near the middle of the keyboard have two, and the higher ones have three strings each. Any one of these strings may become relaxed and cause the tone to lose its proper pitch.

After the piano has been used moderately for a year, it should hold its pitch for about six months. Newer pianos need to be tuned at least once every three months. Many concert pianists have their pianos tuned before every performance.

Strobe Tuning

A new system of tuning developed and used in recent years is called "strobe tuning." It involves an electronic device carried by the piano tuner and plugged into an electronical outlet while he tunes the piano. Small alligator clips connect each string, one at a time, to the unit. By striking a particular key, the tuner can ascertain whether or not the string is sharp or flat. He brings it into the proper pitch in much the same way as the manual tuner.

This system is rejected by many concert pianists, but lauded by others. I perfer it to manual tuning, if a tuner is not an expert.

Knowing the Make-up of the Instruments

Every music director should have some knowledge of the technical make-up of the instruments, especially the piano. Often he is called on to purchase a used piano; therefore, he should know what to look for in a good used piano. This calls for some knowledge of the instrument. Although it is not necessary for him to master this information, some music directors have done so and can tune their own pianos. The basic elements of technical piano knowledge would include the relationship of the string to the bridge, soundboard construction, the striking of the hammers. When purchasing new or used instruments, counsel should be sought from technically knowledgeable men such as the piano dealer or the tuner used by your church.

Most organs, whether electronic or pipe, will give years of service under proper care and treatment. Here are a few points to know and remember.

Be sure to turn off the switch when the instrument is not in use. Any musical instrument should be played only by those who understand and appreciate it; careless use might damage it. As with any electronic instrument, the organ should be handled with care. Stop tabs, keys, and pedals should not be slammed or jammed down, just played or used normally.

While the organ can be moved to suit the church, adequate help in moving it should be obtained, to prevent personal injuries or damage to the instrument. Be sure the pedal clavier is properly removed or adjusted, the cord unplugged, and the cable connection removed enough to permit the desired adjustment. The pedal clavier may be removed so that the console may be moved or cleaned, but the slots must be well seated when it is replaced, so that each contact can be made properly.

The use of transistors in the newer organs has saved a world of technical repair and simplified the job of the service technicians.

Except for taking care of the finish, keys, and pedals, do not try to service an organ yourself. If an organ has not performed properly, the dealer should be called so that prompt attention can be given. A minor adjustment or replacement can turn into a major repair job by overanxiety combined with curiosity.

To clean the stop tabs of an organ, slightly moisten a lint-free cloth and rub gently back and forth. If plain water does not suffice, a limited amount of mild soap may be added. Use this same procedure on the keys; rub gently and dry with a soft cloth.

Before calling a serviceman for problems with the organ, there are a few things you might check whether:

1. The organ is plugged into an electrical outlet.
2. The outlet is working.
3. The main organ switch is turned on.
4. There is current coming through the organ switch; a fuse in the organ or the electrical system may be blown.
5. The stop tab on the manual you are trying to play is depressed or engaged.
6. When you press the expression pedals back and forth, a normal increase in volume is obtained.
7. The connection between consoles and amplification equipment is proper.

If you cannot get the proper performance from your organ after checking these points, a serviceman should be called.

Locating and Enlisting Proper Service Departments

Make sure that a professional organ repairman or piano tuner is called to service your instruments. Aspiring electronic "geniuses" can add more problems than help, because of a lack of experience and knowledge of the particular instrument. A would-be repairman, though proficient in servicing many other electrical instruments, may be at a complete loss when trying to figure out the intricacy of your organ console. His experimentations may result in serious and expensive repairs.

Soon after purchasing a used organ, the proper service department should be located so that prompt and efficient repairs can be made. This is usually taken care of by the company from which a new instrument is purchased.

Proper Cleaning of Cabinets and Consoles

The casing of your instruments, or the cabinet, as it may be called, is a beautiful piece of furniture and can enhance the decor of any church interior, but it must be properly cared for. Because the life expectancy of these cabinets and consoles is so long, a great deal of research and technical know-how has gone into their development and manufacture. They require little care, other than proper dusting and cleaning, which should be done according to the instructions of the manufacturers or dealers.

Temperature Change and its Toll

Extreme heat or cold may damage the finish of an organ. Sudden changes of temperature or excessive changes in humidity also may injure it by instantly affecting the moisture content of the wood case parts, even though they are carefully coated with lacquer. Swelling or shrinkage may crack or chip the finish.

Do not place the organ over a heat register, near a stream or a hot-water radiator, or near an outside window that might be open for any length of time. The same holds true for the piano. Extremes of heat or cold cause the piano to lose its proper pitch rapidly. The strings will swell or contract with the changing temperature; this is true of a new piano more than older instruments.

Regulations for Playing the Instruments

Any church needs new talent developed through the years and should encourage younger musicians to practice. The organ may be made available for such practice but should be regulated with care. Many instruments are absolutely ruined because children are allowed to "bang" on them before and after services. If the organ is left open so that "whosoever will" may come in and play at any time, the result is usually that the instrument is left on to overheat or to suffer damage.

An organ or piano dealer can have locks put on your instruments, so that the proper regulations can be instituted to care for them.

23

The Music Council

IT has long been my opinion that a music director should work directly under the pastor; that is to say, he takes instructions solely from the pastor, not from a music committee or music council. However, a properly operated music council has great merit. Members are not selected to choose the direction of the music program or to stand in judgment of the music program. Neither are they to select the persons to help in the music program. They are to do no hiring or firing. But there are several aspects of the music program with which they can be a decided help.

Duties of a Music Council

1. Plan the calendar for the music program of the church at the beginning of the year.

2. Help find sources for music arrangements.

3. Make suggestions and help choose music helpers, such as children's choir directors, pianists, choir mothers.

4. Make suggestions concerning performances. This is probably the most vital aspect of the work of the music council. In its

sessions the group tries to determine new and different ways to present special music in the church services, especially with the choir.

Following is the list of ways to present the choir numbers, compiled by the Music Council at the First Baptist Church of Hammond, Indiana, under my direction. Pencils and paper were distributed, and each council member listed as many different methods and ways to present a choir number as he could think of. After five minutes, each person was asked to present his methods to the whole group. This list is the result of that five minutes of thought by the Music Council.

Ways to Present a Choir Special

1. A choir with an accordion accompaniment
2. A portion of the arrangement sung by a mixed quartet
3. A choir accompanied by a trumpet trio. The trio can be used in interludes also.
4. A choir with a violin obbligato
5. An arrangement with an a cappella passage
6. An arrangement done completely a cappella
7. A choir arrangement with a solo passage
8. A Western type choir number with guitar accompaniment
9. An arrangement presented by the men's section of the choir
10. An arrangement presented by the ladies' section of the choir
11. A man's chorus with soprano obbligato
12. Antiphonal singing. An octet or slightly larger group may sing from the back of the church or from the balcony with an echo effect.
13. A trio with choir background
14. A choir arrangement with a section sung by six ladies two on each part.
15. A choir number with a men's duet in one passage
16. The use of a snare drum with a patriotic song or choir arrangement
17. A portion of the arrangement sung by a men's quartet

18. A medley of songs
19. A passage sung by a mixed trio
20. A passage of the arrangement sung by the men's section a cappella
21. Soprano solo with choir background
22. Alto solo passages in the choir arrangement
23. A choir arrangement featuring solo passages with the organ and piano
24. A selection by the choir with a deaf person singing a "solo part." This is an interpretation of the song, but done very beautifully
25. An arrangement with a mixed duet singing one passage
26. A Negro spiritual
27. The choir presenting a new number from the hymnal
28. The congregation joining with the choir in singing a special number
29. A teen choir in the balcony singing along with the adult choir in the choir loft
30. A choir arrangement with one passage featuring the ladies in three-part harmony
31. A missionary song with a short passage in Spanish or some other foreign language
32. Multiple solos with the choir in an arrangement
33. An invitation type arrangement sung just before the message
34. The choir arrangement starting in unison, building one part at a time until singing in four-part harmony
35. An arrangement with special effects on the organ

This gives you some idea of the freshness that can be experienced by the congregation with the unique presentation of choir numbers planned and discussed with the Music Council.

Choosing a Council

The total church family should be represented on the Music Council. It should include at least two people from the congregation, the pianist and the organist, the music director, and at least one representative from each section of the choir. There may be others; this group does not need to be large, but representative.

The Value of Having a Music Council

If a Music Council is selected and used wisely, the result will be a fresher, more delightful music program, with added variety. Imagine the thrill of a congregation that can walk into the church auditorium expecting to hear something new and different and exciting each time the choir stands to sing. Variety is the spice of any music program. May God help you to use more than one head (yours) in planning for and creating a music program that will honor Christ.

24

Building for Church Music

A LARGE percentage of church services is taken up with music, yet when some congregations build new auditoriums, they do so with little or no regard for the music program. There are many things that the ordinary layman is not aware of, that are necessary to assure the best music. The building committee should consult with experienced music directors when planning for a new building campaign. This chapter deals with many of the factors that should receive consideration.

Choir Rehearsal Room

It is not always possible to have an extra room designated as the choir rehearsal room, but, with planning, this can be done without additional expense. This room can double as a classroom, but also be an excellent choir rehearsal room. Most choirs would not think of rehearsing during the Sunday school hour, so there would not be any conflicts. If it is possible to have a choir rehearsal room, several features should be provided.

Duplicate Seating

The room should be large enough so that seating in the choir room can duplicate the seating in the choir loft. This allows the music director to have his choir in the same position during rehearsal that they are in while performing.

It also allows him to seat them and find out which seats will be vacant during the church service. If rearrangements are necessary or substitutes must be recruited at the last moment, this will be indicated by the empty seats in the choir rehearsal room, prior to going into the service.

Music Storage Space

Any choir that sings regularly in the service will have need for storage space for music that is being performed weekly and needs to be repeated periodically.

This music should be kept in good order so that the music director can quickly put his hands on it. A music director may have to change his plans at the last moment; therefore, he needs to be able to quickly run through his music files to find additional music.

Choir Clothing Storage Space

There should be ample space for storage of robes, capes, blazers, and dresses that are used by the choir members. These storage spaces should have sufficient space around them so that many people may have access at the same time. This storage space should be as near the seating area as possible.

Acoustics

Acoustics in the choir rehearsal room should be the same as in the auditorium. When the choir is rehearsing, the acoustical sound should be the same as when the church auditorium is filled with people. This may require deadening in certain areas, because most church auditoriums are more "dead" than the choir rehearsal rooms. Usually the ceilings and the walls are hard in the smaller room, and the sound bounces back more rapidly, giving a very "live" sound acoustically, as opposed to the live sound, period.

The choir will feel much more at ease on the platform during the performance if they sound, to themselves, much as they did in the choir rehearsal room. On the other hand, if in the choir rehearsal room they can open up and sing with gusto because of tremendous resonance, they may become intimidated when transferred to the choir loft without that same resonance. Most people, when they can hear only their own voice, are intimidated. In the rehearsal room they were able to hear the voices of others so much more dominantly, they were not timid about joining in without reservation.

Room Location

The rehearsal room should be as near the auditorium platform as possible; an ideal place would be directly behind the pulpit area. This allows the choirs to take their positions prior to the service in the rehearsal room and then file out directly into the auditorium. This prevents a mix-up in seating or improvising in the entry way outside the choir loft. Anything that helps to put the audience at ease should be done; the audience will feel much more at ease if they sense that the choir is well rehearsed and know exactly where they are supposed to stand or sit.

Organ Tone Chambers

One area lacking in many churches is the organ tone chamber. The organ sound will be much bigger, more pleasing, and more widely distributed if the organ tone chambers are engineered properly and installed as the building is being constructed.

A good installation will result when an even intensity of tone is provided to three principal groups: the congregation, the choir, and the organist. The tone chambers should be positioned to cover the room and the groups mentioned above with even, undistorted tone. Most major organ dealers have technical knowledge and can provide many helpful suggestions for proper installation of the organ. They should be brought into the picture before the construction starts, so that they can call attention to such things as conduit for wiring, etc. Consider the following additional aspects of tone chambers.

The tone chambers should be of a size sufficient to give proper amplification to the tone for the size of the auditorium. Any organ dealer of the major companies would have proper information concerning this. The opening should be large enough to allow a minimum of twelve inches for clearance on both sides and top of the cabinet. If the choir is situated behind or to one side of the main opening, another opening should be made facing the choir. The opening for the choir should be equivalent to the main opening, or slightly smaller if space is limited. Two cabinets without sufficient tone openings will sound subdued and bottled up. The front and side cabinet openings can be covered with an appropriate grill. In a large chamber where more than one tone cabinet will be installed, the openings for the cabinets must be made larger. One tone cabinet may be placed on top of another, provided a felt or sponge-rubber pad is placed between them. Moreover, when a large installation is planned, it is advisable to stagger tone cabinets all over the church or auditorium. It is usually desirable to place tone cabinets in one general location, such as at one end of the auditorium.

The walls of the tone chambers should be hard, enabling the room to amplify the sound and diffuse it somewhat, thereby rendering a pleasing and distant effect. It is advisable to remove all sound-absorbing material from the room in an installation of this kind. The tone cabinet inside the chamber should be on a stand or supported sturdily. The components of the tone cabinet will need attention, so it is important to provide easy access to the cabinet.

In the majority of church installations the location of the tone chambers will be governed by custom. The chamber should be located so that the organist receives its tone directly without its being too loud or too weak. The tone should sound at the same level to the organist as to the congregation. The choir should hear the sound from the tone chambers over and above the sound of their own singing voice without any acoustical obstructions.

A good rule to remember is that the tone chamber should be placed so that the immediate sound is above the heads of the congregation. There should be as few physical obstructions as possible between the tone cabinets and the audience. Precautionary measures should be taken to assure ample distribution of sound throughout the listening area. Especially in large churches and auditoriums, the tone chambers should be located near the console.

Acoustics in the Auditorium

Many believe that it is almost impossible to have an auditorium that is acoustically ideal for speaking and also for music. Acoustical engineers have almost totally conquered this problem, although it may remain a problem in churches where short cuts are taken or where there are false conceptions concerning acoustics.

To have a heartwarming, lifegiving service, congregational singing must be vibrant and alive. This is absolutely impossible in an auditorium that has been deadened acoustically with acoustical plaster on the ceiling, carpet completely covering the floor, and acoustical fabrics or materials on the walls. Padded pews also add to the deadening effect. This can be overcome with expensive public address systems, but nothing can take the place of natural, bright musical tones receiving the proper amount of amplification in a well-designed auditorium. The reason that many churches have poor congregational singing is that they are so dead acoustically that each person hears himself singing much louder than his neighbor; therefore he becomes intimidated by his own voice. He quiets down, so that others may not hear him. With everyone doing this, the congregational singing is absolutely ruined.

If acoustical plaster or other materials are used on the ceiling, then it should be omitted directly over the choir and a hard surface substituted without fail. The wall directly behind the choir should be hard, so the sound can be amplified and transmitted back to the audience. It is better to have a parabolic curve behind the choir, so the sound can be thrown in a straight line from the back wall to the auditorium.

Now, consider some materials that might be placed in an auditorium to deaden or decrease the acoustics.

Carpet

Carpet is most desirable on the platform and in the aisles, but, by all means, don't install it beneath the seats and in the choir loft. It is absolutely unpardonable and unforgivable to put carpet in the choir loft, thus causing the choir to have to sing their lungs out to be heard. Carpeting will also greatly diminish the congregational singing and therefore hurt the service. The carpet on the platform and in the aisles should not be thick plush carpet, but should have a very smooth surface with as little deadening as possible.

Padded Pews

Many acoustical engineers feel that padded pews give the same effect as a full auditorium. This is true, but on Sunday evening and Wednesday evening when most congregations are not filled, the smaller crowd needs the acoustical help of the hard surface on the back of the pews that are not filled. The pews in the congregation may be cushioned without too much damage, but the backs of the pews should be left hard. The choir seating should be hard-surfaced without exception.

Acoustical Ceilings

High ceilings with materials that retain the sound give absolutely no help to the congregational singing or to the speaker.

Therefore, a great deal of thought and planning should go into the ceiling. Under no circumstances should the ceiling under the balcony be of acoustical materials. It is much better to have an auditorium that is too "live" than to have one that is too "dead," because a live auditorium can be very easily deadened, but a dead auditorium can only be helped by putting in expensive public address equipment, and that will only help the speaker and the musicians on the platform. The congregational singing will suffer greatly.

Piano Placements

The space provided for the piano should be adequate to care for a grand piano; especially is this important in a larger auditorium. In an auditorium seating one thousand or more, space should be provided for a concert grand piano; even though a piano of that size is not used at first, it may be desired in the future, so space should be available.

If the auditorium is dead, a PA system will be needed for the piano; therefore, the conduit should be run in the beginning stages of the building so that microphones can be placed in the piano pit, preferably under the piano on a short stand.

Planning Should Start with the Architect

A time to start planning for the music is when the first conferences are held with the architect, so that he knows exactly what you are looking for in the way of sound for the music program. Most architects are not musicians; therefore, any information that they have along this line comes from experience or from a service. Do not depend on them to provide for the music, because too often they are guilty of leaving the music program out of the picture. Many times the building is built, the furnishings are starting to go in, and, all of a sudden, unfortunate people realize that they have not planned correctly. Don't let this happen to you.

25

Helpful Hints for

the Music Director

CONSIDER at this point twelve "do's" and twelve "don'ts" for a good music director. In order to end on a positive note, let's take the don'ts first.

1. Don't neglect preparation. The choir can immediately sense when the conductor is ill prepared for the choir practice.

2. Don't organize the complete music program all at one time.

3. Don't lead the people faster than they are willing and able to follow. Give them time to digest what you have already given them.

4. Don't criticize the music director who preceded you.

5. Don't make too many sudden changes.

6. Don't organize all the choirs at once. Start with the adult choir and get it to rolling smoothly. Then move quickly on to the teenage choir, the Junior choir, and the children's choirs.

7. Don't let criticism discourage you.

8. Don't let your personal ideas and tastes dominate the complete music program. Consider the likes and dislikes of others in your planning of the music.

9. Don't overlook the other departments of the church work. Realize that the people who are involved in the music program are also involved in other areas of the church work, and they must give some time to other responsibilities. Try not to cause their loyalties to be divided or force them to choose between two positions in which they are serving Christ.

10. Don't forget that you are working with all kinds of people.

11. Don't allow your time to be used by too many duties outside the church.

12. Don't lose the spirit of humility.

Now here are twelve do's for a good choir director.

1. Always be sincere about your work.

2. Develop confidence in yourself.

3. Be friendly to everyone.

4. Develop vitality.

5. Develop a good music ear. Many times a music director has to really work at this. This does not come naturally for some people.

6. Display real joy in directing the choirs.

7. Be flexible at all times. Try to come to the place where you can make changes smoothly in the middle of a service.

8. Learn to mold an audience, encouraging their participation in the music program of the service, thereby preparing them for the pastor's message to follow.

9. Have a sense of humor. Be able to laugh at yourself.

10. Be ever learning.

11. Keep a good Christian testimony.

12. By all means, be a soul-winner.

Here are several other tips that will prove helpful to music directors in most situations.

1. Make sure the pianist and the organist can see all of the platform, so they can watch every move that the director makes, and make sure they do watch.

2. The first word of the choir number is most important. If the first word is strong and full of assurance, the audience relaxes. They sense that you know exactly what you are doing, that you

have practiced well, and they will enjoy and be blessed by the choir number.

3. Don't call attention to mistakes or difficult passages. If a person in the choir makes a mistake, just pretend for the moment that it didn't happen. Ask the choir members not to nudge each other, or to call attention to themselves during difficult passages by frowning or shaking the head.

4. Ask the choir not to chew gum or talk, distracting the audience.

5. Ask choir members to be careful of bored or concerned expressions. Many times the attitude of the audience is set by the facial expressions of those in the choir. Tell them to "enjoy the services and make sure it shows on your face."

6. Have the choir open the services. It seems that every service can be started a little better with a vibrant opening choir number. It should be a short, special arrangement of a chorus or the refrain of a gospel song or hymn.

7. Always have a good ending on every choir special. If there is a good beginning and a good ending, the audience seems to forget most of what went on inbetween. To be sure of an effective ending, spend a great deal of time practicing it.

8. Have the choir rehearse at least one verse of the congregational numbers for the following Sunday at each rehearsal. This does two things: (1) It allows them to better lead the congregational singing; (2) It helps them to warm up and get ready for the practice of the special choir arrangements.

9. Urge the choir always to sit and stand erect. Nothing looks more slouchy or careless than choir members sitting on the tip of their spine or standing in a leaning position. Besides giving a poor appearance, they cannot sing or perform well in such a position.

10. Teach the choir to sing in a relaxed manner, with the mouth open wide vertically, to produce better tone quality. It softens and mellows the harsh tones.

11. Choose good rehearsal times, when most of the members can be present. Sometimes it is better to rehearse after the Wednesday night service; sometimes it is better on a special night.

The adult choir at First Baptist Church of Hammond practices from 7:00 to 8:30 on Thursday evening, and from 6:15 to 6:45 on Sunday Evenings. The teenage-choir rehearsal is from 5:00 to 6:00 on Sunday afternoon. The Junior, Primary, and Beginner Choirs practice from 6:30 to 7:15 on Wednesday evening, during the teachers' and officers' meeting.

12. Always try to vary the program a little bit; make sure it is vibrant, alive, and evangelistic. When people hear your choirs sing, they should sense that they believe what they are singing. This can only be true with an evangelistic music program. Anthems and classical sacred music are good; but be sure that everything in the service leads to soul winning, warmth, and Christian love.

26

Music Fundamentals

for Choir Members

SOMEONE has said that music is a language understood by all mankind. How true this is. Many times we are moved by music when nothing else seems to touch our hearts.

Music, good music, is a gift from God and should be regarded as such. Only God can give man the beautiful melodies that we have today. Man has, in many cases, with his corrupt and evil mind, dragged music through the mire and caused some of it to be a thing of disgust and to be shunned by Christians. Yet on the other hand we still have God-given sacred music that should be regarded very highly.

Every song that we sing in church services should be sung with an air of reverence to God. Many of the songs that we have came as expressions of the hearts of men to God as they were moved by the Holy Spirit.

There is much said in the Bible concerning singing and praising God with song. A favorite scripture text is Colossians 3:16, "Let the Word of Christ dwell in you richly in all wisdom; teaching and admonishing one another in psalms and hymns and spiritual songs, singing with grace in your hearts to the Lord."

MUSIC FUNDAMENTALS:

I. Main elements of music—All music falls into one of these three.
   A. Rhythm—This deals with the timing or lengths of tones and how often they occur.
   B. Melody—This is the tune. (A continuation of tones one after another in a desired pattern.) All music is built around the melody.
   C. Harmony—This is a combination of two or more tones sounded together that produce a pleasing effect.
II. A tone and its make-up—A tone is a sound with a definite pitch. This is caused by regular vibrations. A tone may be musical or non-musical, not good or bad. A tone has four characteristics.
   A. Length—long or short
   B. Pitch—high or low
   C. Power—loud or soft
   D. Quality—sad, joyful, firm, etc.
III. The departments of music
   A. Rhythmics—the lengths of tones
   B. Melodics—the pitch of tones
   C. Dynamics—the power and quality of tones
   D. Theory—the principles and rules of music
IV. Notes and Rests
   A. A note is a figure used to represent the length of a tone. Its position on the staff determines the pitch on the tone.
   B. A rest is a figure used to represent the length of silence in a musical passage.

Notes are as follows: Rests are as follows:
   𝒐 A whole note   ▬ A whole rest

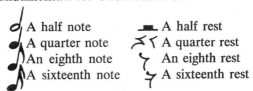

A half note	A half rest
A quarter note	A quarter rest
An eighth note	An eighth rest
A sixteenth note	A sixteenth rest

A dot following the note gives the note its full value PLUS ½ of its value. For example: A ♩ gets 2 beats while a ♩• gets 3 beats.

V. A *MUSIC STAFF* consists of five parallel, horizontal lines and four spaces.

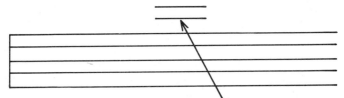

A line above or below the staff is a *ledger line.*

A *score* is one or more staves that run across the page and are joined by a vertical line called a *brace.*

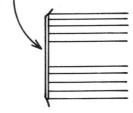

There are three kinds of clefs.

1. Treble clef — ladies' voices

2. Bass clef — men's voices

3. Tenor clef — men's voices

Each staff is divided into *measures* by *measure bars*.

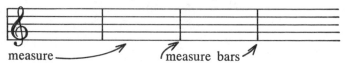

measure ————————→   ⌒measure bars ↗

Each measure has an equal number of beats in it according to the rhythm of the song or selection of music.

VI. Division of Voices:

1. Soprano — ladies — high voices
2. Alto   — ladies — low voices
3. Tenor   — men   — high voices
4. Bass   — men   — low voices

Women sing ONLY soprano and alto.   Men ONLY sing tenor and bass.

VII. Time signatures:

At the beginning of each song is a TIME SIGNATURE which tells how many beats are in each measure and which note gets one beat.

Examples: $\frac{4}{4}$ $\frac{3}{4}$ $\frac{6}{8}$

The TOP number tells the number of beats in a measure, and the LOWER number tells which note gets one beat.

Example:

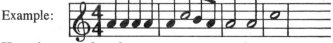

Here there are four beats per measure and a quarter note gets one beat.

VIII. Key signatures:

At the beginning of each song there is a KEY SIGNATURE which tells what key the song is in. It tells which notes are to be lowered and which are to be raised according to the key of the song.

A flat (♭) lowers the note ½ step. A sharp (♯) raises
the tone a ½ step. A natural (♮) cancels any sharp or flat.

Major key signatures:

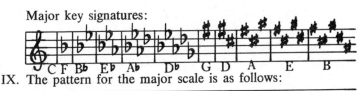

C F B♭ E♭ A♭ D♭ G D A E B

IX. The pattern for the major scale is as follows:

½   ½ (1–whole step)(½–half step)

X. Musical Terms:

Dynamics:
1. pp (pianissimo) very soft
2. p (piano) soft
3. mp (mezzopiano) moderately soft
4. ff (fortissimo) very loud
5. f (forte) loud
6. mf (mezzoforte) moderately loud
7. (crescendo) gradually get louder
8. (Decrescendo) gradually get softer

Tempo:
1. largo—very broad
2. lento—slow
3. allegro—fast
4. presto—very fast
5. andante—walking tempo
6. accelerando—get faster
7. ritard—get slower
8. tempo—lively
9. legato—smooth and connected
10. staccato—(♪) separated and cut short

Other musical terms:
1. A capella—to sing without instrumental accompaniment.

2. Coda—a closing phrase added to a song.
3. Formata—(⌢) hold as long as the conductor indicates.
4. Falsetto—a false tone that is considerably higher than normal.
5. Obligato—a higher melody used as accompaniment or harmony to the main tune.
6. Staggered breathing—individual choir members breathe at various times to give a continuous flow of music.
7. Unison—entire choir sings the melody in comfortable singing range.
8. Slur—(♪♩) moving from one tone to another, touching inbetween tones.
9. Repeat—repeat music between the repeat signs.

10. Phrase—a short passage of several measures of music.
11. Resonance—amplification of a tone to give it quality.
12. Chord—sounding of two or more tones together.

SONG LEADING:

Almost any person with a love for good songs and a sense of rhythm can lead congregational songs. There are a few simple patterns, which, if used correctly, are universally accepted.

The hand movements of a song leader are definite patterns, if done correctly, and not just wild gyrations. You can learn these to great advantage. They must be practiced over and over until they become a part of you, just as walking or talking. The more you practice the easier and smoother the patterns become.

I. PATTERN FOR SONGS IN 4/4 TIME AND 12/8 TIME.

Pattern:

Sample songs:
"Nothing But the Blood"
"Standing On the Promises"

The down beat or "1" beat on the first note after each measure bar. This is how you tell you are keeping the right time.
Each song should begin with a PREPARATION BEAT.

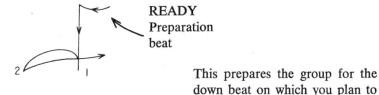

READY
Preparation
beat

This prepares the group for the down beat on which you plan to begin.

Many times a song is started with a part of a measure or on the 4th (last) beat of your pattern. The preparation beat should be first, then the beginning beat of the song, then the down beat (first beat of your pattern).

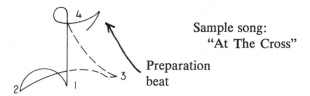

Sample song:
     "At The Cross"

Preparation
beat

II. PATTERN FOR SONGS IN 3/4 TIME, 9/8 TIME, AND 9/12 TIME.

Sample songs:
     "Amazing Grace"
     "Faith of Our Fathers"

The principles and rules are the same as for 4/4 time.
III. PATTERN FOR SONGS IN 6/8 TIME AND 6/4 TIME.

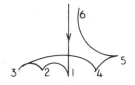

You may use two 3/4 patterns in each measure of a song in 6/8 time or 6/4 time.

Other patterns that can be used for 6/4 or 6/8 time, especially 6/8:

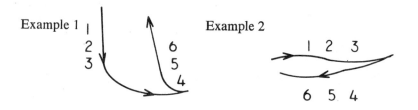

Example 1

Example 2

Pattern for 2/2 time:

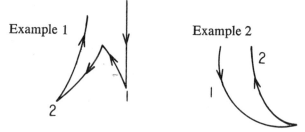

Example 1

Example 2

When you are about to lead a song, consider these factors before beginning:

1. What is the time signature?
2. What pattern should I use?
3. On which beat do I start?

Always try to be at ease and comfortable while leading a song. BE YOURSELF!